ENDORSEMENTS

Before reading Gary's book *Crazy in Love*, I knew there must be more to God than normal church, worship and prayer but was struggling to break through and find that true relationship I could feel pulling on me. From the very start and all the way through this book, Gary poured out such deep revelation of God's love and His original design for our intimate relationship. Now, I no longer doubt how unconditionally I'm loved, and I've also stopped striving, which has brought such peace and confidence to my purpose and everyday walk with God. *Crazy in Love* changed my life.

— JOE BLOUIN, PRESIDENT, BLOUIN GROUP, INC.

As people find themselves on a continual quest to discover what it means to be loved, valued, and accepted, Gary leads them to the ultimate source for all three—the intimate heart of God. Having known Gary for many years, the message of this book is the driving passion in his life. As you embark on the journey of understanding that you were created for love, you will experience the reality that God has captured your heart and that you have captured His. Enjoy getting to know your "Bridegroom King." It's a journey worth taking.

— Eric Foust, Campus Life Pastor, The Stirring

It was a privilege for me to share Crazy in Love with our staff at Youth With A Mission Northwoods. I couldn't wait until it was published to share it with them. We all enjoyed the nuggets of truth that we gleaned as we read together. Gary's writing and lifestyle have been an inspiration to me. The chapter titles, "First Things First," "The Chase is On," "Will You Marry Me", "Is God Enough" are each a thought for the day in themselves. They have the potential to realign you with God's intentions for your life. The way Gary shares about intimacy with Christ makes it something to be grasped rather than just a pie in the sky idea. You will be challenged and magnetized into the heart of God as you read this book.

— David Holmbeck, Oasis World Ministries

Crazy
in Love

Crazy in *Love*

Igniting Passion and Purpose
In Your Relationship with Christ

Gary Chiles

Dwell Book Press

To order more books or to learn more about the author, please visit the author's website:

www.GaryChiles.com

I dedicate this book to my wonderful wife of over 30 years, Beth. Your belief in me and this message is the reason this book exists. I understand Christ's love better because of you! Thanks for being the best friend I could ever ask for. I love you.

And to my children, Lily and Leland. You light up my life!

CONTENTS

ACKNOWLEDGMENTS

Eric Foust – Thanks for taking a chance with me 20+ years ago and giving me an outlet to process this message.

Dave Holmbeck – Thanks for your friendship and our late night conversations about the romance and passion of God.

Bob, Joe, Mark, Zack – Thanks for all the lunches, coffee and phone calls and for being a part of this journey with me.

Mom – Thanks for giving me a heritage of faith for the impossible.

Dad – Thanks for being an example of diligence in the work place and of loyalty in friendships.

Jack & Sharon Johnson, my in-laws – Thanks for always believing in me and putting up with my bad jokes.

INTRODUCTION

Most of my early Christian life was a struggle—a painfully exhausting struggle. My spiritual life became a never-ending, complicated list of dos and don'ts, always trying to please God who actually seemed somewhat unpleasable. This cycle of displeasure, appeasement, and perpetual questioning whether He was angry with me or not was fatiguing. Yet, I had this small flicker of hope that there had to be more. Please God, let there be more! But when I questioned or doubted the system, I was told to pray harder, give extra and spend more time reading the Bible. Instead of giving me hope, this caused even more frustration. I felt like I was running on a hamster wheel going nowhere fast, which led to boredom and burnout. Was this seriously what Jesus meant when He said, "Follow me"?

As time passed, the desire to make sense of life intensified. I wanted to know why I was created and why He loved me (whatever "love" meant). These questions came to a head when I went to Bible college, where I hoped and prayed I would find all the answers to my nagging questions. But instead, the hamster wheel kept spinning. Though the school and training were beneficial, I left with even more uncertainty, and more questions than answers. There was still a big gaping hole in my heart that theology couldn't fill. Later I served God in ministry, hoping this would fill me up somehow. But the quest to understand the "why" of life continued to gnaw at me. Why did God start this grand experiment called life? With all of the struggles in life, what was the point? What was on His heart when He created me?

As my search continued, I kept bumping into standard theological answers, which only widened the void in my heart. What I seemed to hear, in one way or another, were cure-all answers that didn't address my nagging questions. First, "You are a sinner, so repent!" While this is true and repentance is vital, I also had the gut feeling that God did not create us only to repent. Now what?

The next response I would often hear was, "Go and serve God! Find out what God has called you to do, and that will give you a sense of purpose, solving all your problems." So I hopped on that treadmill for a while (more than once, actually), but still to no avail. Instead, I just got more tired and frustrated. What now?

"You must have more sin in your life, so repent even harder, and then do even more for God. And don't forget that Jesus died for you, so you owe Him! Oh, by the way, He loves you." In some twisted way, that made me feel a little better for a moment or two, but then it would leave a bitter taste in my mouth. Repent and serve God; rinse and repeat—repent and serve God. I heard it over and over in a variety of ways, so it must be right—right? It all sounded so spiritual, so how could I argue? Is this all there is to life?

Spiritual boredom and burnout started to feel normal.

~

Then I discovered a treasure, or maybe the Treasure discovered me. Either way, it rocked my world. I realized that I was created for something greater than just repenting and doing good works, and that there was more to my relationship with God than being His servant or His child. I encountered a verse in the Bible, Hosea 2:16, which took me on a quest that changed my life. Through this journey, I unearthed the answer to the big "why" of life—the reason I was created. This revelation astounded me! It gave me new confidence in my relationship with Christ, which transformed everything about how I lived, prayed, and read the Bible. Even more importantly, I understood more clearly how He truly sees me.

I wrote this book for those who know there is still something missing, something wrong with the status quo. And amid the confusion of life, the cry of your heart is crystal clear: "There has to be more! Please God, let there be more!" This book won't answer every question, but it will provide some basic tools to start climbing out of the pit of a mundane and unfulfilling Christian existence and into something exhilarating, meaningful, and life-changing. Join me on this remarkable treasure hunt to discover why He is crazy in love with you!

1

THE HEARTBEAT OF GOD

B elieve it or not, romance is the heartbeat of God. It is the central theme and driving force of creation itself. From the beginning of time, God designed us to be the object of His love and affection. Astonishingly, He also created us to have the freedom to love Him back—or not. He designed the world to contain this two-way relationship between our Creator and His creation. This joint relationship is a love story—the first and grandest of its kind.

Amazingly, the one thing God would never do is force someone to love Him, otherwise it couldn't be called love. God's plan from the beginning was not to be a dictator, barking out orders to His lowly servants like an overbearing control freak. Likewise, He did not create us only to save us and show off His mercy. God had something much more majestic on His mind. He wanted to take the biggest risk He could ever take: to create a people with the freedom to choose whether to love Him or not—to choose a face-to-face relationship with Him or to reject Him and walk away. Love is the greatest risk of all!

Woven into the fabric of every love story on earth is God's DNA. Please catch this: the very spark of creation is in each romantic thought and idea. This is why romance impacts our hearts in such a deep way. God never designed us for a generic, common, everyday love. Instead, He uniquely fashioned us for the most intimate and personal love relationship one can ever experience: marriage.

Have you ever heard a love song that was so amazing and beautiful that it felt, in some strange way, spiritual? Or what about a romantic movie you didn't want to end because you were captured by the passion between two people that seemed perfect for each other? This would happen to me, but it felt awkward. I could never put my finger on these uneasy feelings. To start with, romance wasn't a comfortable topic for me, especially in my younger years. Then add God to the equation and things grew even more confusing. How can these two worlds ever be combined together?

I grew up in church where it was scandalous for "secular" music and movies to cross paths with God. I had no grid for anything in the secular world to be able to reach me spiritually. I was told that anything connected to the "world" was off-limits; it was unspiritual and evil if it didn't come from the church. This caused me to feel guilty if something from the world could move me. Yet at times, I could sense something mystical and special watching two people connect on screen that stirred me spiritually somehow. I couldn't deny that *something*—or *Someone*—was pulling at my heartstrings in ways I couldn't explain.

For years, I've been intrigued by the emotional impact love stories have had on my life. Whether it was in movies, books, or music, the dream to live "happily ever after" with someone has always captured my heart. And I'm not the only one! Why is this such a universal desire? Year after year, generation after generation, many movies, books and songs present the same question: Will two strangers who meet capture each other's heart? Will they survive adversity to live happily ever after?

I must confess: I love "love" stories, especially when the guy gets the girl at the end of the movie and they ride off into the sunset together. It feels so right to see this happen. This seems to be the way life is supposed to be: perfect couple = happy life. Even though many people have tried and failed to find "true" love, they still chase the dream—or at least they like to watch a movie about it. This is why perfect movie endings are so idyllic and sell so well to the audience; it's a dream that lives inside of our hearts, inside of our spirit. We don't know why, it's just there. And even if these "happily ever after" stories are too good to be true, we still want them to happen, somehow, to us. Why is that?

The "perfect love" portrayed in movies and books is but a dimly lit picture of His perfect love

There is a cry in the human spirit for the perfect movie ending. It is a cry deep within the core of every human being, men and women alike. All people want to love and be loved by someone special, someone with whom we can be ourselves with, someone who fills us up on the inside. On some level, even the hardest, crustiest people have these same cravings as well. **We all long for the dance of romance.** At times, we might find a taste of it in the natural world, and it feels good when it happens. But at the end of the day, worldly romance still seems strangely empty and temporary, leaving us craving for something more. Even if we do find our soul mate and experience amazing love, as time moves on, we realize that there is still some kind of longing that human romance can't satisfy.

This cry in the human spirit for romance is actually a God-designed longing. It's an eternal longing! This God-given yearning is a pathway to something better, something truer; something that will satisfy the deepest part of the soul. The "perfect love" portrayed in movies and books is but a dimly lit picture of His perfect love, His perfect desire towards us. *Jesus is inviting us to live "happily ever after" with Him!* Now that's a great love story! We love perfect endings in movies because we were created to experience THE perfect ending. (Sadly some are still looking for it in all the wrong places.)

When I finally grasped this divine design for life, it answered many of the questions I had about life and satisfied the emptiness in my spirit. It radically changed the way I saw Jesus. Let me repeat: *it radically changed the way I saw Jesus.* I finally realized that my inner longings had a higher purpose behind them. I was able to get off of the "Repent and serve God" merry-go-round that religion kept me on. As I discovered the intimate—dare I say, the romantic—side of God, I started to comprehend the real reason we were created. And it was a lot different than what I was taught in Sunday school.

I know this may sound overdramatic to some, or too simplistic to others, but this is a life-changing truth: Jesus wants to know *me!* He wants to be with *me!* And not just as a servant or a child, but as His cherished lover, His betrothed bride. At first, this truth scared me; then it intrigued me. Finally, it drew me into a journey that changed the way I do life forever.

God did not create the world so that He could sit back and watch us struggle on earth, waiting for us to figure out the right things to do to make Him happy, or at least a little less cranky. What a terrible creator that would be! Instead, He designed this world for a much higher purpose, and it all started in the garden of Eden.

God's courtship with humanity began when He created Adam and Eve. He was madly in love with His creation, and still is! He loved spending time with them, taking walks "in the cool of the day" (Gen. 3:8), developing a deep and lively friendship with them both. This single-focused desire in God's heart has not changed, and it never will. It is as strong as ever.

God created this grand experiment called "life" in order to have the chance to live happily ever after with us. He risked it all, even going to the cross, in order to experience something special and unique—a two-way love affair. Jesus didn't suffer just so we would be rule-abiding robots who would simply obey His every command. What a bore that would be. Instead, He wanted free-will human beings who have the choice to say yes or no to experiencing this bond of love. God wasn't trying to start a religion, but a relationship.

God wasn't trying to start a religion, but a relationship

Through the study of the Word, I discovered He doesn't want just any type of relationship with us, but one that is so close and intimate, the only picture worthy of comparison is that of marriage, where two become one (Eph. 5:31–32)—this is the longing of God! The whisper of romance we hear in music, read in books, and watch in movies is a prophetic invitation—a marriage proposal—asking us to say yes to Him so we might experience something more in life: *a romance with Christ.*

2

THE WHISPER OF ROMANCE

Then He said, "Go out, and stand on the mountain before the
Lord." And behold, the Lord passed by, and a great and strong
wind tore into the mountains and broke the rocks in pieces before
the Lord, but the Lord was not in the wind; and after the wind
an earthquake, but the Lord was not in the earthquake; and
after the earthquake a fire, but the Lord was not in the fire; and
*after the fire a **still small voice.***
—1 Kings 19:11–12 NKJV, emphasis added

Deep down inside each one of us is the still small voice of the Holy Spirit, telling us there is something more to life, something more meaningful. Even though it's quiet, it's persistent, calling our hearts to go deeper. But in the insanity of life, it's not recognized or heard very well. Instead it can feel annoying, almost intrusive. We might not mean to feel this way, but we just do. Sometimes we can almost hear an opposite voice inside shouting back, "Leave me alone. I'm fine where I'm at. Please quit bothering me." And all is well, for a moment.

If we are listening and truly honest with ourselves, this voice might bother us at times. It has the ability to get under our skin, telling us there is something missing in our lives. This voice often comes when our thoughts are the quietest and most vulnerable, like in the middle of the night or early in the morning when life is still. Pained by this unsettledness, it's easy to stifle the un-comfortableness by turning on music or the TV, reading a book, or surfing social media. We try to stay busy doing something, anything to escape this unquenchable gnawing.

Yet through it all, no matter what we do, the whisper continues. In our lack of spiritual self-awareness, we sometimes don't even realize how much our hearts are crying out for something more. We thought that saying yes to Jesus cured all of those needs, not knowing that that was just the beginning. But in God's amazing grace, He uses this still small voice to help reveal the deep needs and desires in our soul before we even know it's there. And when we listen to His whispers, instead of finding condemnation and disapproval, we find quite the opposite. He always points us to the unfathomable treasures of intimacy.

Ignoring this *"still small voice"* has caused me a lot of pain over the years. There was a subtle yet constant under-current of turmoil in my life. Even though I went to church, prayed, and read the Bible, something was still wrong, but I could never put my finger on it. I thought salvation was supposed

Even though I went to church, prayed, and read the Bible, something was still wrong

to be the answer to everything, and yet the emptiness continued.

Then in my mid-twenties, life took an unexpected turn. It started one Sunday morning at a church where I was the youth pastor and adult Sunday school teacher. A visiting missionary from Chile came and spoke at my Sunday morning class that day. He opened his message by telling us he wanted to talk about something he was just starting to explore in his spiritual life. The missionary explained that he didn't have all of the answers yet, but he knew there was profound truth in this subject. The topic was romancing the heart of God.

When he shared this, it felt like God shot an arrow into my soul. *Romancing God's heart—what was that? Did I hear him correctly?* I felt side-swiped by this. I was expecting a totally different message. Missionaries usually emphasized the need to serve God and win the world for Jesus; I was ready for that. But this was something new and it took me by complete surprise.

As I sat there listening to his message, questions started to flood my mind: *What does this look like? Why would God want us to do that? Did this mean God wanted to romance my heart as well? Was this even scriptural?*

I was perplexed yet intrigued. Romance and God were two words that didn't seem to fit together. As I pondered this message for a time, I knew something fresh was beginning to awaken in my heart, but I didn't know what to do with the concept of a romance with God. The churches I attended didn't address this subject. It was exciting but confusing at the same time. Unfortunately, after some time had passed, these questions subsided, and things went back to normal. The idea was a seed planted that went dormant in my heart for a season.

As time went by, I came across a few nuggets of gold here and there on this topic that would stir my heart for a moment or two, then evaporate, leaving me searching for more. Though I couldn't express it then, I now realize I was searching for answers to two main questions that would define my spiritual journey: First, who am I to God? And second, who is God to me? As I was finding the answers to these two questions, I inadvertently solved the age old "why" question for me: why was I created. Getting this settled in my heart changed my spiritual DNA forever. This search for (and discovery of) something deeper ruined me for all the usual religious answers.

This search for something deeper ruined me for the usual religious answers

The tipping point happened a few years later when the Lord used two key avenues in my journey to spark a change. One, which I will discuss in a later chapter, was studying Hosea 2 (as well as other key passages in the Bible) for the first time in my life. Digging deep into the context and meaning of these verses caused a seismic shift in my theology, which then changed the way I daily related to Jesus. Through this passage in Hosea, I began to understand more of who am I to God and who He is to me. After more than twenty years of researching this topic, I'm still stunned by these revelations in His Word. (Again, more on this later.)

The second thing He used to soften my heart and instigate change was strangely enough, music. While most of my awakenings were happening through the study of the Word, a few special songs were doing something different inside of me that hadn't happened before. The most notable experience I can remember happened when I stumbled upon a CD, *Winds of Worship, Vol. 3.* I was surprised how the Lord used a couple of songs from this album to awaken the cry in my soul for something deeper than what I had before: It was the cry for intimacy with God.

The lyrics were bold, almost scandalous—like the words in Song of Solomon:

> *Let me know the kisses of Your mouth; Let me feel Your warm embrace; Let me smell the fragrance of Your touch; Let me see Your lovely face; Oh, take me away with You; Even so, Lord, come; I love You Lord; I love You more than life.* [1]

Even though the words felt awkward and uncomfortable at first, a holy hunger for something new and fresh awakened. A new sense of His presence and closeness stirred inside of me. It felt like icebergs were melting my frozen heart. Something transforming was taking place.

This music was like much-needed water pouring over my parched soul. I played these songs repeatedly with my eyes closed, letting my heart become softened and romanced by Jesus. I even started to re-connect with some secular love songs, singing them back to Him, where before, I would have been too religious to even think about doing that. I started to feel saturated in His love in a fresh way. Out of this renewal, worship, prayer, and Bible reading took on a whole new meaning for me. Instead of being a religious obligation, they became part of my growing relationship with Him.

Since that time, even though my journey with Christ has been full of ups and downs, I knew things were different and that I was building a new foundation, one that finally started to make sense. I had a new purpose in my walk. I started to gain a new view of Jesus and understood with new clarity His view of me. I finally discovered a treasure worth selling all for (Matt. 13:44).

~

On this journey, I realized something critical: What we are missing in life is a love affair with our Creator—yes, a love affair. I'm talking about *the* love affair of all love affairs. He created us first and foremost for this one purpose. God did not create Adam just so He would have a full-time gardener— He wanted intimacy.

Please let this sink in: *God created us for intimacy.*

God did not create us just so He could save us. He did not create us just so we would serve Him forever—what a short-sighted God that would be. Instead, He created us to have a lifelong, love-filled relationship with Him. This changes the foundation and reason for everything that we do, including our service for Him. Please don't miss this: Our Creator designed us to enjoy a two-way relationship with Him forever. Pure and simple.

This understanding changes everything. It gives new meaning to life. Unfortunately, the church in general has replaced *communion* with God, with *activity* for God. The purpose of creation has been muddied and distorted; the love affair that He desired from the beginning of time has been exchanged for the legalism of do's and don'ts—this is the foundation of religion. Let me repeat, God wasn't trying to start a religion.

God did not create us just to save us

The truth of the matter is this: All God ever wanted was us. Can we let this in? Let me make this more personal: All God ever wanted was you! We have a not-so-secret admirer and some don't even know it. We might even sing "Jesus loves me, this I know" and still not recognize how madly in love He is with us! He is outright Jealous for us—for that is His name (Exod. 34:14). The sad thing is that we are usually content with a casual meeting with Him once or twice a week, and maybe a peck on the cheek. But guess what? There is more! He wants more! That's the part that scares me and yet captivates me at the same time. And if you quiet yourself, tune your ear to those yearnings inside your heart—and really stop and listen, you will recognize that your heart wants more, too.

My prayer is that the whisper of emptiness will drive us to His whisper of romance!

This book is for those who are not satisfied with their current walk with Christ. You know deep down that there must be more to following Him than just going to church on Sundays and following all the correct rules. If you are like me, you are surrounded by a lot of people with all the "right answers," but something is still missing; something is still wrong. You know that His still small voice is calling your name, but you are not sure how to answer.

But amid all the confusion, the cry of your heart is crystal clear: "My spiritual life is empty; something is missing and I have to have more!" This is my attempt to put words on paper that may help define and add some context to this longing for more.

Lyrics from an old John Fischer song expresses my heart best:

I'm not one who's got it all in place, telling you what you should do; No, I'm just one old hungry beggar, showing you where I found food.[2]

3

THE VOID FACTOR

The phrase "God-shaped vacuum" or "God-shaped hole" has often been used as an illustration to describe the emptiness we have in our hearts before coming to know Jesus as our Savior. We tell others that after accepting Jesus into our hearts, this vacuum will finally be filled. The truth is, we are filled to some extent. But is the void ever completely gone?

Growing up in the Christian community, on the average, I saw little difference in the lives of people who claimed to know Christ as their Lord and those who did not. From an early age, this troubled me. Those who professed to have a relationship with Jesus seemed just as unhappy as those who didn't know Jesus. They were stressed about the same things, struggled with the same sin issues, and got angry and upset over the same circumstances. In the big scope of life, Christians seemed to have little or no more freedom and peace in their lives than those who weren't Christians. And I was no different.

There was endless drama in the church as well as outside

of the church. In my early years, this was embarrassing and caused me to pull back from wanting to share my faith with others. What could I say? "Come to Jesus, and in about fifty or sixty years, you will go to heaven—but until then, good luck to you! Not much else in your life will change. You will have little or no more peace than you do now. But, hey, you can't have everything, right?" What kind of deal is that?

The hard questions before us are these: Why doesn't saying yes to following Christ fill the hole in our hearts once and for all? If the void is supposed to be gone, why do we still struggle with emptiness? These are difficult questions that need real answers.

If the void is supposed to be gone, why do we still struggle with emptiness?

I would like to suggest that when we first meet Him, God *does* fill the inner void, but only in a partial way. There are times in our Christian walk when we are set free from certain bondages and sins, and we experience transformation and freedom in those areas. But why doesn't that solve the problem of emptiness and unrest over every part of our lives?

What I am about to describe took years for me to grasp, but as time went on, it changed my life.

～

The first thing I came to realize is that God purposely built into the fabric of our lives a void—an emptiness—that our possessions, jobs, ministries or hobbies cannot fill completely. These things are satisfying at first, but only to a certain degree. In His wisdom, God carefully put hidden limits on how much inner life we can pull from this life in order to protect us.

Shortly after buying a new car, moving to a different house, or starting a new job, the twinge of emptiness comes. Even in our relationships, after the infamous "honeymoon" phase is over, the void begins to creep back in, little by little. The people we meet, the things we buy, and the choices we make promise so much at first but deliver so little. Even serving God has this little hole in it. And before we stop long enough to realize the letdown, to feel the sting of these unfulfilled promises, we quickly move on to something else, or someone else—something new and more exciting. The merry-go-round continues, and we miss the purpose of the barrenness.

~

One night, this void became very real in my life. As I mentioned before, I went to Bible college right out of high school, but kept hitting a spiritual wall. So I quit and re-started school a couple of different times, trying to figure things out. After dropping out of college for the second time, I found a decent paying job, married my college sweetheart, moved into a nice condo in a nice suburb of Minneapolis, and bought two new cars. So there I was, a poor farm-boy from Iowa in my early twenties, already reaching some small milestones of "success" in the big city, much to my surprise.

One beautiful spring evening as I was standing out on my deck, I caught a glimpse below of one of the new cars I had just bought. I started to reflect on all my blessings, including my beautiful wife and all of the things I owned—when out of nowhere, a weighty feeling of emptiness hit my spirit. This description might sound ironic, but that's what it felt like. I can still remember my spirit flinching as it struck me. I felt the impact, not in my emotions per se, but somewhere deeper inside. I tried to shake it off in the moment, but couldn't. This foreign feeling just sat quietly in the background of my emotions.

As I was trying to process what had just happened, I felt something missing. With my little bit of success, I was expecting to feel some type of satisfaction and contentment, but there was nothing there. It was just an empty, blank feeling. All of this hard work, and I couldn't sense any pleasure from it. To say the least, I was bummed.

What intrigued me later (and fueled a lot of what you will read in this book) is that about two years later, I jumped back into ministry and really focused anew on my spiritual growth. But I could still feel this empty pit in my stomach pop up from time to time (especially when I was trying to climb the ministry ladder). Going to church more and working hard at ministry didn't ease that vacant feeling I had. There was still something missing.

Somewhere in my early teens, I discovered the book of Ecclesiastes and was intrigued. Years later, as I processed this experience on my deck through the grid of Ecclesiastes, the only way I could describe what hit me that evening was something I now call the "still small voice of emptiness" —which ironically was a springboard for me to recognize His "still small voice of intimacy" later on in my journey. I believe we all have both of these voices whispering to us; it's just a matter of whether we hear them or not.

⁓

I always hated that little uneasy feeling deep down inside, that little inner itch that wasn't quite satisfied when the excitement of the day's events wore off. Even though I was good at covering it up at times, it was always present at some level. Over time, I realized that God was whispering through this uncomfortableness and pain a really big truth: spiritual yearnings can't be touched by physical pleasures. Please catch this: spiritual desires, needs and longings cannot be satisfied by the things of this world. I know this may sound elementary, yet I believe that many struggle with this more than they will admit.

But this takes honesty to recognize. It takes being spiritually still to pin-point the uncomfortable feeling inside. The "void factor" in our lives is very small but powerful. The sense of emptiness just sits there quietly in the background; it doesn't yell or scream, but lurks around in an annoying way. I am amazed at how easy it is to ignore the twinges of emptiness. Why is that? Maybe we are afraid to stop and listen. Maybe we are afraid of realizing how big this emptiness is in our lives. But if we listen, if we turn our ear to it, it can become a giant compass pointing to spiritual freedom!

Does this mean we aren't supposed to enjoy the external pleasures of life? Of course not! Many religious zealots have tried to make the enjoyments of life evil and off limits. This is so unfair to God. The creative God of the universe wants us to enjoy His creation! He wants us to enjoy life! But we were created for a bigger purpose than temporary pleasures. He designed us for eternal pleasure—to enjoy a friendship that will last for eternity. And this enjoyment can start now. We don't have to wait for heaven!

But God knows that we have a tendency to allow the addictiveness of natural pleasures to pull us away from experiencing eternal pleasures. When this happens, desiring more of

His friendship becomes less important; intimacy slowly erodes into the background and becomes more of a fairytale—something that seems unreal or unattainable. Then the enemy of our soul wins by keeping us on the endless treadmill of trying to satisfy spiritual longings using earthly methods. This allows the unending dramas and disappointments of life to bombard us to the same degree as unbelievers because we don't know how to live in the secret place of His protection (Ps. 27:5).

It took me years to actually appreciate the purpose of this void. Instead of being a thorn in my side, it was actually a huge blessing. This led me to the next big realization.

~

So why does God allow this void to exist in our lives in the first place? Why does it cause so much uncomfortableness and pain, even after we start to follow Christ?

In His infinite wisdom, **God uses emptiness as a spiritual protection device.** It's His way of trying to keep our spirit safe with Him. Let me explain.

Romans 8:20–21 says, *"For the* **creation was subjected to futility (condemned to frustration—** AMP*), not of its own will,* **but because of Him** *who subjected it,* **in hope that the creation itself also will be set free from its slavery to corruption into the freedom** *of the glory of the children of God"* (NASB, emphasis mine).

In His infinite wisdom, God uses emptiness as a spiritual protection device

God's goal is always for us to be *"free from … slavery"* and live in total freedom. He wants us to experience the pleasure of abandoned friendship with our Bridegroom, which is the foundational purpose of creation! But He also knew that because of our brokenness, we would be constantly prone to pulling too much life from the things around us—thus the need for *"futility."* **The sting of futility is God's attempt to keep us from being swallowed up by the temporary.** It's God's warning signal to our hearts—if we choose to listen to it.

God created us with the capacity to enjoy the pleasures of life—a high capacity at that. But even though this is a God-given ability, **natural pleasures were never designed to satisfy us spiritually**. Why? Because if they could, we would have little or no spiritual appetite; we would have no desire for anything beyond what we can see, taste or touch in the natural world. In other words, if we could satisfy spiritual longings using physical pleasures, we would be able to spend money to find inner rest, or we could eat our way to true spiritual peace (believe me, I've tried it—doesn't work!). The fact is being a millionaire will not protect you from emptiness. God is jealous to be the only one who can satisfy your innermost being.

God made it illegal for our spiritual appetites to be satisfied from natural resources, no matter how good they are. Without futility built into the fabric of life, there would be little to no reason to search for something deeper with Jesus. One of the biggest roadblocks to enjoying the eternal side of life on a regular basis is our addiction to the temporary side of life—thus our need to feel the irritation of emptiness from time to time. This is God's protection device; He's protecting love; He's protecting intimacy. If we recognize this as God's grace, then we can learn to balance the external side of life with the eternal side in a healthy way.

Sadly, most of us aren't taught how to identify and navigate these two areas in our hearts. I know I wasn't. Without realizing it, we try to satisfy our eternal desires—the longing for intimacy with Jesus—with external solutions. We don't mean to, it just happens. In the busyness of life, in the brokenness of life, we ignore the subtle Godly hunger pains and settle for something less special, less satisfying. Then emptiness quietly creeps in; the empty pit deep inside starts gnawing on us. It's here at this intersection we have an opportunity to stop and listen to His "still small voice"—or reach for the TV remote, the credit card, or fill in the blank. **God's goal is to use the pain of emptiness to get our attention focused on something bigger, something better.**

~

This leads to the last important cornerstone on this topic: it's important to understand, and navigate, the differences between the external and eternal areas that live inside each one of us. Understanding a few basic principles around this helped me conquer one of my biggest spiritual battles and laid the groundwork to grow in intimacy. Let me explain.

Even though I always knew that we have a soul and a spirit, I didn't pay much attention to the difference between them. When I would hear these terms mentioned in a teaching, nothing stood out as important to me; it all blended together in my mind into one big happy family. I rationalized that if there was a problem with one side of this equation, it usually affected the other side as well, so why bother with all the little details in-between; just get it fixed and move on. It wasn't until my battle to find real inner rest and peace came to a head that it became crucial to discover these differences.

And the fruit of this discovery had a domino effect in other areas of my life as well.

This is not an exact science, but let me try to un-blur these two areas as best as I can in a practical way (if it isn't practical, then it's just useless theory). This is not meant to be an in-depth theological discussion, but just some simple, and hopefully life-changing, observations.

We know that we have a soul and a spirit. Some people try to get really theological about the differences between these two, but I have often found their explanations of little value in my day-to-day struggles (again, if it isn't practical, it's useless theory). So for my own sanity, I simplified things in a way that was easy to remember and understand. Simply said, we have two areas that coexist on the inside of us—the external (temporal) side and the eternal (spiritual) side.

The "external" describes the normal, routine thoughts and feelings we have on a day to day basis. This is where we spend most of our time in our thought life—it's our "natural" way of thinking.

The "eternal" part is our spiritual side that lives just beyond the external, just beyond our natural thoughts and feelings. It's important to note that the eternal or spiritual side can still be felt by our natural senses, kind of—if we pay attention to it, but it's just a little bit different. In other words, we can feel our spiritual side, but not really, yet we can —sometimes. This gets tricky trying to describe this on paper, but let's continue.

The important part is this: the eternal part is a special place God created deep inside our inner being that is separate and distinct from the external part of us. This special, yet separate place, is not where we experience the natural pleasures and pains of life. Instead, it's a quiet, hidden area where His still small voice of affection dwells; it's where we can freely access His incredible rest, peace, joy, and friendship at a moment's notice—if we know it's there. In Psalms, David describes this as "the secret place" of intimate refuge (Ps. 27:5; 91:1 NKJV).

Here is one of the most critical parts to grasp: as a follower of Christ, the eternal area is a place in our hearts where His presence lives whether we feel it or not! Let me repeat—**whether we feel it or not!** When this truth becomes a reality in your heart, the enemy is in trouble.

We all have this eternal part hidden inside, but many of us don't know how to recognize or find it in a practical way. Because I wasn't taught much about this topic, I never gave it much thought. I would sense the Lord's presence from time to time, maybe during a good church service or prayer time, but then it would go away—it was like the wind, coming and going as it pleased. I assumed this was the normal way of walking with God, waiting for the wind to blow so you could "feel" something. Then when it would pass, I would pray, trying to convince God to let it happen again, but usually to no avail. Eventually I assumed that only super spiritual people could conjure up this feeling on a regular basis.

It wasn't until my battle to find consistent inner peace, that I started to connect the dots and realize how important it is to recognize the differences between what I could *feel* for a fleeting moment verses what was *real* on a consistent basis

~

Truths that are born out of a battle are the ones that mean the most. Learning what peace really is and how to live in it on a consistent basis is one such truth to me. The battle to find true rest was a huge milestone for me; it has had major ripple effects across my whole spiritual life. The best part is that it helped create a firm foundation for friendship and intimacy that was missing before.

While it's impossible to detail all of the bumps and bruises around this journey, let me try to describe the basic points that changed my life.

In Philippians 4:7, Paul describes God's peace as that *"which transcends all understanding"* (NIV). I used to gloss over this passage, thinking that because His peace *"transcends all understanding,"* it must be hard to find; it must be in outer space somewhere, only accessible to the super-spiritual. I thought that the un-written rule was if I could muster up enough spirituality and jump high enough on the religious trampoline, then maybe—just maybe—I could get a taste of this "peace" somehow.

Peace was always a carrot dangling off a long stick, just beyond my reach. I rarely felt spiritual enough to reach it, which put even more distance between me and this mysterious feeling. If I happened to be in a desperate situation, I would make another run for this unreachable carrot—then collapse in spiritual exhaustion once again when nothing happened. I lived frustrated and confused, searching for peace but seldom finding it. And if I did "feel" something, it was gone before I knew it.

God's peace lives inside of me, whether I feel it or not

After years of struggling, I finally discovered a truth that changed everything! It helped me find—and maintain —peace in a practical way. I realized that God's peace lives inside of me, whether I "felt" it or not! How do I know this is true? Because He lives inside of me (whether I feel Him or not), and He is peace. Please let me repeat this: He is peace! (I know this may sound simple, but the inner battle to live this out is very real.) Not only is Jesus the Prince of Peace, He is peace in the flesh!

When I came to the realization that God's peace is a Person and not an emotion, my life changed. I quit trying to chase a feeling and started to pursue a Person. . I didn't have to be a victim any longer to my whimsical mood swings any longer (this deserves a hundred exclamation marks!). I finally discovered that peace was there all along, but I was looking for it in all the wrong places.

Here are the dots that took me a while to connect, but helped cement this truth in my life: when I began to realize that God's peace does not originate in my feelings (the external part of me) but in the One who lives in me (in the eternal part of me), I had to change. I had to train myself to quit looking to my natural feelings to see whether peace existed or not. I had to recalibrate my inner process on where to find true rest, but this took a lot of practice and time. This is why it's important to know the difference between the external and eternal areas in one's heart.

Ironically, the more I found real Peace in the eternal part of my heart, the more I started to sense the "feeling" of peace without trying! But now it's just the icing on the cake because He is so much more satisfying than a feeling.

One of the more challenging parts in this process is learning to keep the eyes of my heart focused on Jesus. The important thing I now realize is that when the direction of my gaze is off, I tend to slip into old habits of trying to find spiritual life from natural resources, which then triggers the empty, futile feelings all over again. So I've learned to be purposeful in my focus—my gaze—to avoid the pitfalls that emptiness brings.

I love how Hebrews describes an important step in this process: *"Looking away [from all that will distract] to Jesus...."* (Heb. 12:2a AMP, emphasis added). Sometimes, redirecting our focus is the hardest thing to do, because distractions are so... distracting. But be encouraged: breakthrough is just on the other side of those distractions! The reward of winning the battle over distractions is we get to experience His gaze back towards us. This is where the fun begins. Here is a secret the enemy doesn't want you to know —the more we experience His gaze of affection, the easier this journey becomes because Jesus is very addicting! And this all starts with a glance of our eyes towards His. (Research Song of Sol. 4:9 and 6:5 to gain more insight into the power of our glances.)

As I redirected the focus of my heart towards Him on a regular basis, I sensed things starting to change. Slowly but surely, I began to enter into His secret place of intimacy more freely and naturally, without feeling the pressure to act more "spiritual" to get there. It also wasn't as difficult as I had imagined it to be either. I started by taking a few minutes just to spend with Him; nothing complicated or super spiritual. Then I made this a part of my life, just like spending time with my wife. Jesus is not a religious experience, but a Person who enjoys being with me.

Likewise, I discovered that I could access His peace anytime I wanted (whether I felt like it or not)—because He is inside of me (whether I feel Him or not). I didn't have to jump through a bunch of spiritual hoops to find Him! I am learning that I don't have to be a slave to my up-and-down emotions any longer. If my emotions start to get turmoiled, instead of being out of sorts for hours or days on end, I've learned to re-group more quickly; I just have to stop and shift my focus back to Him. It's like the "stop, drop, and roll" fire safety technique taught to minimize injury if someone's clothes catch on fire. Spiritually speaking, when things go wrong, instead of panicking and running around like I'm on fire, I have to STOP and re-direct the gaze of my heart back to His gaze—and that is where I find protection (Ps. 91). Although the process is simple, it's not always easy, especially when your "clothes" are on fire. But with practice, this process is a game changer.

Remember, if you feel like peace and intimacy are a million miles away, be encouraged because they are not, because He is not! His secret place is inside of you and He is excited to spend time with you there anytime you want!

~

When understood, the voids of life are a gift from the Lord. They can become stepping stones to deeper levels with Him. The more we can be still and identify the "still small voice of emptiness" ironically, the easier it becomes to identify His "still small voice of intimacy." In God's wisdom, these two areas in the heart are like two sides of one coin, connected together to allure us closer to Himself.

If there was anyone who understood the pain and purpose of futility, it was Solomon. As one of the wisest men in Scripture, he tried a grand experiment. He sought to find meaning and contentment in this life without a relationship with God. His experiment failed (which actually made it a success.)

Holding nothing back, he wrote an honest book about this failure: Ecclesiastes.

Solomon's grand conclusion is wrapped up in this stark passage:

> *"Meaningless! Meaningless!" says the Teacher. "Utterly meaningless! Everything is meaningless."* (Ecclesiastes 1:2 NIV)

Some view the main essence of Ecclesiastes as bleak and only relevant for those who do not know Christ as their Savior. I disagree. Its truth and wisdom are relevant for everyone.

If we don't understand the difference between the external and the eternal parts inside of us, and if we don't understand the purpose of the *"meaningless,"* then Solomon's conclusion can be discouraging, even depressing. But it doesn't have to be. God's goal in Ecclesiastes is not depression, but freedom!

It is no coincidence that the book of Ecclesiastes precedes the book of Song of Solomon, an amazing allegory of the love affair between the Messiah (Jesus) and His bride. There is a powerful connection between these two books. After years of pain and struggle, then finally tasting something that turned my world upside down, I have come to this conclusion:

One cannot truly taste the depths of an intimate friendship with Jesus as described in the Song of Solomon until one has truly understood the depths of the emptiness of life described in Ecclesiastes.

God's goal in Ecclesiastes is not to kill the enjoyment of life, but to propel us into life-changing intimacy with Jesus. The God-designed emptiness keeps us hungry for something more; that something more is a deep, eternal friendship with Jesus!

My prayer is that these two books, Ecclesiastes and Song of Solomon, will become the "bookends" to your spiritual journey. **May the frustration and emptiness of life thrust you into the bottomless depths of His love and passion for you!**

4

LOVE ME OR ELSE?

Jesus replied: "Love the Lord your God with all your heart and with all your soul and with all your mind." This is the first and greatest commandment.
—*Matthew 22:37–38 NIV*

How do you command someone to love? And how do you command someone to love God with their whole heart? This impossibility caught me off guard one day as an unfair and seemingly lopsided challenge. How is this possible? Yet this is what Jesus commands us to do: *"Love the Lord your God with all your heart and with all your soul and with all your mind"* (Matt. 22:37 NIV; see also Mark 12:30; Luke 10:27; cf. Deut. 6:5). This command is a daunting task! It would be hard enough to do if it were merely a suggestion or a good idea, but it is not. On top of that, Jesus also raises the stakes by declaring it to be the "first and greatest commandment"

(Matt. 22:38). How am I supposed to fulfill this lofty obligation?

The irony is this—love cannot be commanded. Love cannot be forced. Love must be a choice, otherwise it cannot be called love. Trying to command love is as absurd and useless as a prison guard ordering a prisoner to "love" him or be punished. The one being threatened may say the words and act a certain way to avoid penalty, but the intent is meaningless. Jesus did not die on the cross just to demand a forced confession out of us. So what is this command really about?

This command to love God is actually quite profound. We usually associate commands with *doing something*, but this one is unusual because it involves *knowing Someone*. **The first command is not something you obey, but someone you become—a lover.** God is not saying, "You better love me or else!" while holding a big stick behind His back, waiting to smack you if you don't comply. Instead, He is inviting us into a life of friendship and intimacy, to experience the freedom of surrendering all of ourselves to the Lover of our souls: Jesus.

This is a huge change in thinking, especially for those who try to earn brownie points from God by following all the right rules and regulations to make sure He's pleased with them. This is not a dry, stale command from your "boss" in heaven. He is not pointing a long bony finger in your face, telling you to do more, try harder, and climb more walls to prove your love for Him. That is religion, not relationship. You cannot "accomplish" this command but only be changed by it. It is an invitation to life, not to more rules. The first commandment is alive because He is alive.

The first command is not something you obey, but someone you become - a lover

There is a hidden twist to this commandment that if understood, would free us to live with a lot more abandonment. *The first command reflects God's personality and desire toward us.* He loves us with His whole heart! The first commandment is a mirror of love personified—Jesus. It describes how He acts and feels towards us—and how He longs for us to act and feel towards Him. If we truly understood this, we would read and understand the Bible through a whole new lens.

The first command reflects God's personality and desire toward us

God is not some insecure, tyrannical prison guard looking for meaningless words and actions from a prisoner. Instead, He is looking for an equally yoked bride. He wants us to feel what He feels toward us. He wants us to see Him as He sees us—as a lover. This is why Jesus calls the first commandment the greatest commandment of all.

Here is what's fun about this journey: As we start to experience a little bit of this romance (it might be just a glance of His eyes or a small taste of inner peace), something amazing starts to happen. We will want to have more. We will *have* to have more! Romance is addicting! Instead of being stressed trying to obey this command, He wants us to encounter it. He wants us to *experience* the reality of it with our whole hearts, not just read about it in the Bible! The important thing is to take it one step at a time, one day at a time, and watch your spiritual life change.

~

Experiencing the first commandment takes time and patience. But we must realize that the ability to grow into this lifestyle of love—made possible only through God—is not guaranteed. Saying "Yes" to Jesus does not automatically make you a lover. Love must be a choice, otherwise it can't be called love. The definition and foundation of love is built on the freedom to choose. It is our responsibility to respond to His love and His constant wooing of our hearts. It is also our responsibility to be vulnerable to the call of intimacy, or intimacy can't be given. Jesus wants us to ask, seek, and knock for this (Matt. 7:7; Luke 11:9). In return, He wants to provide His help and power to do the impossible—to love Him with *your whole* heart. But like in any marriage, you must want this to happen.

But there is a balance to everything. Some people translate the idea of God making the impossible, possible, to mean: "It is out of my control; I'm off the hook. I have no say in the matter. If God wants to be closer to me, He knows where I am." Have you ever tried that logic with someone that you are in a relationship with, especially a spouse? Did you ever try a "Que sera, sera" (whatever will be, will be) attitude with this person? How did that work for you? The belief that it is all up to God is totally off base. We always have the power to choose —to say yes or no to a closer heart connection with Him. As in any relationship, drawing closer to another requires desire, commitment, and effort. This is why Jesus is always looking for the hungry of heart (Matt. 5:6).

Others go in the opposite direction. They try to do something right or pleasing to make this commandment happen, thinking that they must prove their worthiness and love to God. They overwork themselves trying to earn what they already have—His love. This, too, is out of balance. Sadly, we either shrink from our responsibility or we take on more than is required. Therein lies the tension. Like in any marriage, we will always have to fight for balance.

In this fight for balance, it can be very easy to miss the first step of this journey—the simplicity of *asking* Him to radically change us. Just ASK! It is really that simple (see Luke 11:9–13). God never ignores this prayer for change. Sincere, heartfelt, persistent asking, *not just the casual want*, draws us closer to the Lord more than we can imagine. Asking causes us to realize our helplessness in obeying this command by ourselves. The first commandment is given to humble us, to break us of our independence and self-centeredness, and reveal the interdependence and interconnectedness He desires with each of us. Pride is not an option. And through this humility, we are given access to the most amazing treasure that exist on earth—face-to-face friendship with Jesus.

                        ⌇

The Christian life is not hard. It's impossible—that's why we need God. —Dave Busby, Evangelist

A word of caution: Too often we attempt to do Christianity in our own strength, without the revelation of who we are to Him and who He is to us (see Hosea 2:16; we will look at this verse in more detail later). This can lead to burnout. As we allow the Holy Spirit to draw our hearts closer to His, we must protect our minds and hearts from the enemy of our soul. Satan will not only try to make us feel condemned and unworthy but also try to complicate things and overburden us. He wants to distract, confuse, and weigh us down so that we will give up the pursuit altogether. As the master deceiver, he likes to whisper in our ear, "Quit trying. It's not worth the effort. True intimacy is not possible—it's just a fantasy. Besides, you have too much sin in your life for God to respond to you. He doesn't even like you. Just give up." Does this sound familiar?

Just remember a couple of things: First, if you are truly open, honest, and surrendered, He is there to meet you. Jesus never condemns—ever (see Rom. 8:1). He only draws you to Himself by the power of His love through the conviction of the Holy Spirit. Second, the seemingly impossible task of giving *all* your love to the One who gave *all* His love to you is possible when you desire it with your whole being. So never —ever—give up the pursuit of this treasure.

~

So I say to you, ask, and it will be given to you; seek, and you will find; knock, and it will be opened to you. For everyone who asks receives, and he who seeks finds, and to him who knocks it will be opened. (Luke 11:9–10 NKJV)

This promise from Jesus is true and is waiting for you! Ask, seek, and knock, and you will enter into the joy of discovering the bottomless riches of the first and greatest commandment.

5

FIRST THINGS FIRST

The noblest rallying cry of the church seems to be to "win the lost," to tell your neighbors about Jesus Christ. Obviously, this is a significant mandate, but is it the most important one?

Not only is this cry usually labeled as the most important, but it also seems to be the hardest to carry out. If it were easy, then every Christian would be doing it consistently. But as it stands, it is difficult to witness and usually with very little results. Why is this?

I believe part of the reason is that we have taken the first and greatest commandment for granted. Let me explain.

Being around church culture my whole life, the message I seemed to hear most consistently was: "Love God, **REACH THE WORLD!**" The emphasis on the second part seemed twice as strong as the first. Sometimes churches skipped the "love God" part altogether, and all I would hear is "REACH THE WORLD!"

On the surface, one may ask, what can be wrong with that? Reaching the world for Christ is a vital aspiration. But when the primary emphasis is on reaching *out*, we inadvertently neglect the supreme importance of reaching *up*.

Being in love with Jesus and discovering why God created us in the first place is often taken for granted, relegated to second place after the great commission. Obviously, we would never say this out loud, but the underlying emphasis puts the first commandment further down the list of importance. If couples did this in marriage—if they prioritized their spouses beneath their jobs, friends, or even their kids, the results would be disastrous. Like in the natural, our spiritual lives suffer when our priorities are out of order. There is a reason the first commandment must be first in our lives!

In some church settings, the first commandment is not the priority; they believe in it, but it's not the driving passion. They preach from a "saved to serve" mentality—meaning, the main reason God wants us in His kingdom is

He saved you for so much more than what you can do!

so that we can obediently serve Him and win the world to Jesus (and grow the congregation in the process). Even though they have good intentions, this subtle shift is wrong; this is not God's design and has unhealthy consequences. This "saved to serve" mentality changes the whole foundation of our relationship with Him.

Instead of being relationship focused, we unintentionally become "doing" focused. Of course, doing things for God is great—that's part of loving others as yourself, which is the second commandment in the New Testament (see Matt. 22:35-40 and Mark 12:28-31). But the "first" must be the first! This is God's design for life.

When the second commandment is out of order, we open the door to very subtle, yet devastating attacks; the enemy turns ordinary questions into direct and poignant arrows that attack our minds and hearts: What are you going to do for God? Where are you going to serve? How much are you going to give? They seem like godly questions, but the source is not.

As time marches on, these questions start to crescendo: Why aren't you doing more for God? Why aren't you serving more? Why aren't you giving more? The pressure to do **more** builds continuously, causing all sorts of spiritual problems (this topic deserves a book all on its own). Unfortunately, when these questions become the focus of our inner world, we can kiss a love affair with Jesus goodbye—and the enemy wins. We become more of a human "doing" than a human "being."

Our view of God becomes warped. We can only think of Him in terms of what He wants from us, not who we are to Him. Inadvertently, we start to view ourselves as someone trying to please a demanding, distant God, who is really hard to please—rather than being a wholehearted lover of Jesus, who is wholeheartedly in love with us! The value and importance of intimacy is downplayed, and sometimes discarded.

Sadly, this unhealthy mentality then spreads to those we are witnessing to. The DNA of striving to "please" gets passed from one generation to another. We reproduce what we were taught.

We need to realize that God saved us for so much more than what we can do.

∽

So how can the church reach the lost easier and more effectively? I propose that it begins by putting the first and greatest commandment back into first place, in the church corporately and in our lives personally. But where does this start?

The first step is simple; it involves asking Him to change our heart's desire—to give us the desire to pursue Him with our whole being. Without this desire, we will just spin our wheels. To think that we can grasp the depth of this amazing commandment (loving Him with all of our heart, soul, and mind) just by reading about it or being told that we should be doing it is a serious misunderstanding. Thankfully, because we were created for the first commandment, Jesus loves to answer this prayer and give us the grace to want more.

This desire for the first command culminates in the ability to pursue or "follow hard" after Jesus. "Follow hard" in the Hebrew language is a unique and descriptive term David used in Psalm 63:8, where he declares, *"My whole being **follows hard** after You and clings closely to You...."* (AMP, emphasis mine). The Hebrew word for this phrase is *dabaq*, which Strong's Concordance defines as "figuratively, to catch by pursuit." We "catch" more of God by pursuing Him. This contrasts the casual glance toward Him on a Sunday, the take-it-or-leave-it attitude that doesn't chase or take hold of anything. **Pursuit is the foundation of all love affairs.**

Whatever you love is what you will pursue and seek after with the most intensity, even if it is costly. A great example is when a young boy falls head over heels in love with a girl for the first time. He is consumed in thought and deed for his one true love. This boy thinks nothing of spending his last few dollars on a gift for her or walking across town just to get a glimpse of her. No cost is too high for the object of his affection.

Pursuit is the foundation of all love affairs.

Most love affairs start with a pursuit, a chase. Without

pursuit, without the desire to go after someone, there is no intimate relationship. And the actual cost of this pursuit (time, money, or energy) matters little, so long as the pursuer catches the one they love. There are no limits or barriers to what someone will do for love.

~

The initial pursuit and subsequent catching of the one we love is just the beginning. The definition of *dabaq* also means being joined together—this is the desired result of catching the object of love. This word is used in Genesis 2:24, which states: *"Therefore a man shall leave his father and mother and be joined (dabaq) to his wife, and they shall become one flesh"* (NKJV). Being joined is the fun and life-changing part!

Paul relates this same concept in Romans 7:4: *"You also have become dead to the law through the body of Christ, that you may be **married** (or **joined**, NASB) to another—to Him who was raised from the dead, that we should bear fruit to God"* (NKJV, emphasis added). Paul clarifies that when we say yes to Jesus and die to our old selves, then we are married to Him. This is huge! Please don't miss this: if we have said yes to Jesus, we are "joined," or married, to Him! I encourage you to please put this book down for a moment and ponder this reality. Forever we are His!

The good news about preaching the "good news" is that the fruit of being married to Christ is reproducing and/or nurturing newborn lovers of Christ. Love naturally produces and reproduces love, without force or coercion.

In the physical world, two people in a healthy marriage naturally reproduce children—the fruit of being joined together. In much the same way, when our love for Jesus consumes us, reproducing (leading others into a growing relationship with Him) is not only easier than before but also enjoyable. When you know God deeply loves you, evangelism (whatever that might look like to you) will flow more naturally. Being a light for Christ in a dark world is a regular part of your life. (And that light can shine in many different ways!)

Likewise, our newborns in the kingdom will be healthier and stronger than before because they are born with great DNA: the first commandment will be first in their lives. They are born out of love, not out of insecure striving to make something happen.

Know this: Jesus said that being yoked or joined to Him was easy, light, and good (Matt. 11:30), but if we are not intimately abiding in Him, we are unable to produce this fruit on our own (John 15:4–5). God never meant for our walk with Christ to be a heavy load to bear. So if your journey is a heavy burden, please examine the foundation you are building on.

~

Fruit is not produced by making fruit an object, nor by thinking of fruit; it is the outcome of having the Lord Jesus as one's object, of thinking of Him. He is the one True Vine who precedes and produces fruit. —Hannah Whitall Smith

As the bride puts herself in the bridegroom's arms on the wedding day and then daily, and as therefore children are born, so the individual Christian is to put himself or herself in the Bridegroom's arms. . . . Then the Christian will bear Christ's fruit out into the fallen, revolted, external world.
—Francis Schaeffer[1]

My Prayer

It's interesting how diverse the landscape of Christianity is today, with more traditions and denominations than I can count. I'm sure my experience is not uncommon, but the denomination I grew up in had this undercurrent to its teaching that made it seem like their set of rules and view of the Bible was better than everyone else's. Unknowingly, this created a lot of spiritual pride and arrogance, blinding me to what the rest of the church had to offer. Even though I might still disagree with others on certain issues, I've learned to respect some of these differences and to see the kingdom reflected through them more than before.

With that being said, I have also become more aware of something else: With all the different theological interpretations and arguments, and all of the various political and social aspirations, the topic of a love affair with Jesus seems to be getting lower and lower on the priority list (of course, this is not true for everyone). The conversation about the first commandment being first appears to be mostly forgotten, distant, muddied. I believe in the search for healthy doctrine and to have accountability when beliefs are false, but please know this: correct theology will not spark a love affair. Something deeper is required!

In some circles, arguing about what's "true" is much more important than intimacy with the Truth; looking down on those whom they disagree with is more satisfying than looking up, catching a glimpse of His eyes. But it's this glimpse that will change a person much more than the "correct" view of the Bible.

My prayer is that the primary, overarching questions we ask as the church changes from, "Do you go to the right church?" and "Do you believe in the right doctrine?" to "Are you in love with Him?" and "Do you realize how madly in love He is with you?"

Revelation 22:17 declares, *"The Spirit and the bride say, 'Come!'"* (NIV). It's not the Spirit and those who win the theological debates that say "Come." Jesus is looking for those who know *who* they are—and *whose* they are. Are you part of His Bride or are you just part of the right denomination doing the right things?

With God's help and His amazing grace, we can change the narrative of Christianity to something higher and more satisfying to our souls. We can call people to a message that will set hearts on fire for the Son of God. We can pivot the focus from *arguing* about Jesus to *intimacy* with Jesus—so we can . . .

. . . *Love God and change the world!*

6

MASTER OR HUSBAND?

I n my life, I knew that I wanted something more. I had to
have more because I was bored and dying inside. I felt
trapped, like I was living in a windowless box with a lead
ceiling that my prayers would bounce off of. Hearing an
endless string of sermons on how to behave better did not
help matters at all.

Then something changed! A light switched on.

One of the biggest milestones in my spiritual journey
occurred when I stumbled on a verse that forever altered the
way I viewed God and completely changed my relationship
with Him. The words jumped off the page, gripped my heart,
and gave me a new understanding of who Jesus is to me:

> *"In that day,"* declares the Lord, *"you will call me 'my*
> *husband'; you will no longer call me 'my master.'"* (Hosea
> 2:16 NIV, emphasis mine)

What an amazing declaration by the Lord! What a radical
statement! This verse—and all of Hosea 2—rocked my world.

The first time I read Hosea 2:16, I kept looking at it to make sure that I wasn't misunderstanding it. *"...you will call me 'my husband'...."* Could this be true? What does this mean? Why didn't anybody tell me about this sooner?

Thankfully, this Old Testament verse with a New Testament promise challenged me to re-examine my understanding of who Christ is to me and who I am to Him. **Hosea 2:16 changed my spiritual DNA forever.**

In this passage, Jesus extends an invitation to all for a level of intimacy with Him that was lost or neglected under the Old Covenant. In the New Covenant, God pushes the reset button.

Jesus wants us to rediscover the foundation for creation.

He wants our relationship with Him to revert to how it was originally designed to be when He walked with Adam and Eve in the garden. Jesus wants us to rediscover the foundation for creation, which is an intimate friendship forever!

∾

Let me expound on this verse a little bit. According to Jewish theology, the phrase *"In that day"* in Hosea 2:16 refers to when the Messiah returns to earth. To the followers of Christ, this is a present-day reality; it is a *now* word because the Messiah is here!

In the phrase *"you will call me,"* the word *"call"* in Hebrew is *tiqrei*. This word is not about the act of calling someone by a name or a title, like "This is my husband, Mr. Smith." It is more meaningful than that. This word *"call"* is connected to the idea of *encountering*. In other words, the Lord is declaring that we can *encounter* Him as our husband. Wow! He wants to encounter me as an intimate friend. This was an overwhelming idea and very hard for me to comprehend at first. But the thought of it also excited me! Buried deep down inside, in a way I couldn't express, I hoped that there was something more to God than the usual religious ideas I was being taught.... Thankfully, there is.

The question we must wrestle with is this: Is this true? Does Jesus want us to encounter Him—to *know* Him—as a husband? Or is this just some religious jargon?

The truth of the matter is this: Jesus is not looking to be known as a task master but as someone who is caring, intimate, protective, and closer than we can imagine. He doesn't want us to view Him through a heavy, oppressive, religious lens but as something completely different and life-changing.

To allow this verse to penetrate our minds and hearts, we need to ask ourselves another question: How do I relate to Jesus—as a husband or a master? If you are like me, you probably didn't know there was even an option. If you examine how you talk to Him and how you hear His voice, I bet you can answer this easily. Is He stern and demanding, or tender and close? When praying, what type of picture do you have of Him? Someone distant and uncaring, or standing next to you, face to face? Do you address Him in a formal manner, not wanting to be disrespectful, or as a close friend?

Take this question a step further: How do I *want* to encounter Jesus? Stop and ponder this. Be honest with yourself and make sure you are even interested in discovering something fresh and new. If you have only known God as your task master, this is a scary thing to think about because it requires giving up your old ways of relating to Him. On the other hand, if you are looking for something more meaningful in your life, this is where the journey toward freedom begins.

The fact of the matter is this: If you want more of Him, you can have it! Jesus always responds to a heart turned toward Him. He is waiting for you. He is excited about you! But if you do not want a closer relationship, He won't force you into one. This is an invitation!

~

Over time, Hosea 2:16 took me to a brand new place in my relationship with Christ that I didn't know was even possible. Through a lot of study and mediation on this passage (and other key supporting verses), a whole new chapter in my walk with Christ opened itself up to me. Before, I thought that walking with Christ meant only being His servant with no hope of anything more. Thankfully, I was wrong.

Please don't misunderstand me: being Christ's servant is part of the journey but now it's in the context of relationship, just like I can serve my wife from a healthy perspective. But the way I was taught was that being a "servant" was the *only* way I could relate to God—the end all, be all of the Bible. This unhealthy view made me feel like I was just a cosmic doormat; God could walk all over me because I am His "servant." No one told me that there was anything higher than this. This left me feeling empty and unfulfilled. I didn't realize that being a servant was only a starting point, not an ending point.

> *Hosea 2:16 took me to a brand new place in my relationship with Christ that I didn't even know was possible.*

I now know that I was created for a greater purpose: to be in a real, give-and-take relationship with my Creator, to love Him and *be loved by* Him (which then takes serving to another whole level). When I realized more was available, I couldn't wait to start exploring all that Jesus had for me. Hosea 2:16 is an invitation to make a radical shift in our relationship to Christ.

∾

Before we go any further, I want to address a very uncomfortable topic for some people—the male/female terminology that is used to describe our relationship with God. We need to understand that the husband/wife language (or Bridegroom/bride terminology) has nothing to do with being a male or a female. Instead, it has everything to do with our *position, posture, and privilege with Him*. Please let this sink in or you won't be able to enjoy this honor to its fullest. This language is referring to how close you can be to the heart of God, not about gender!

In using the marriage metaphor, God was illustrating His passion, His intensity of love for all people.

Men are called the "bride of Christ" just as women are called the "sons of God," which speaks of our position as His heirs. As a man, I do not picture myself as a female before Christ any more than a woman should think of herself as a male son. Paul states in Galatians 3:28, that "there is neither male nor female; for you are all one in Christ Jesus" (NKJV).

I understand that this language can be very awkward and uncomfortable to some, especially for men, but God never meant it to be that way. In using the marriage metaphor, God was illustrating His passion and intensity of love for us. By using the strongest language possible, Jesus reveals how close

He desires to be to us for eternity. It also gives us permission to pursue something deeper than we might have thought possible. So instead of thinking in terms of male or female, think about your position next to Him.

~

Encountering Jesus as Husband was a process for me and it didn't happen overnight. As a logical and pragmatic man, it was hard to wrap my mind around this concept at first. But as I grew to understand the magnitude of what Hosea 2:16 was calling me to, I started to ask the Lord for an understanding of what this meant to our relationship. Slowly, He changed my view of who I am to Him and who He is to me.

Little by little, the Word of God changed my identity. It helped to change the way I connected to Him. I had a new confidence that He wanted to be close to me, even if I wasn't perfect, and that He enjoys being with me (just like I enjoy being with my wife). Prayer and reading the Word took on new life. This new lens changed the way I interacted with Him on a daily basis. Over time, this new identity changed me in more ways than I can describe—mentally, emotionally, and spiritually.

Likewise, as I grew in this intimacy, my old views of obedience have changed. I'm not afraid of disobeying an angry "master" anymore. Instead, I'm excited to follow the Lover of my soul. I talk to Him differently; I listen to Him differently. When I say, "Jesus, I love you!" it means something deeper and more personal than before. My heart is softer and is open to Him in a new way. Encountering Jesus as a Husband was difficult at times, but worth the effort. Thankfully, I will never be the same.

~

Side Note About Feelings

Speaking of difficult, let me take a moment to encourage those who don't "feel" God much, if at all. I grew up in a culture where it seemed that the more spiritual you were, the more you could feel Him. Ironically, some of those who felt Him the most on Sunday seem to have the most out-of-control lives on Monday, which made their experiences with God suspect to me.

Anyway, I was frustrated when I sensed this pressure to feel something in a church or prayer meeting, because usually I couldn't. I would just sit there wondering what was wrong with me. The lack of feelings made me think I was a second-class Christian. I felt left out, hurting what little spiritual self-esteem I had left. And yet I did sense God at times in a very real way—but it wasn't always emotional; it was something different, deeper and below the emotional surface. It wasn't often, but just enough to give me hope that maybe I wasn't totally forgotten.

It wasn't until I found the language and understanding of the intimate *"still small voice"* (1 Kings 19:11–13) that I finally realized that you don't have to "feel" Him in order to sense and know Him. Oh, how I wished someone had told me this sooner. (I covered some of this struggle in Chapter 3.)

The point here is this: most of the changes that happened inside of me were not caused by some big, overwhelming spiritual feeling or experience. Encountering Jesus as Bridegroom was a slow (sometimes painfully slow) process, with some "ah-ha!" moments interjected along the way. Please don't think there must be something big for it to be powerful. This is an unfortunate misnomer that has caused many to miss growth with Him because they are waiting for an earth-shaking moment.

Remember that God's *"still small voice"* in 1 Kings was more powerful than the wind, earthquake, and fire. Never feel intimidated by other people's powerful experiences—sometimes it's God sending a bunch of wind, trying to get their attention; but this is never a substitute for His still small voice of intimacy. (A lot of people make this mistake—then when the "wind" stops, they think God stopped, missing the whisper of His friendship that is always there.) We are all wired differently so we will connect with Him in different ways and at different times. But keep your heart open, knowing that He is pursuing you as a bride, whether you feel it or not.

~

As one starts down the path of discovering the gold in Hosea 2:16, there are many obstacles along the way. There are emotional, mental, and spiritual roadblocks that will come against your spirit as you try to enter a new season with the Lord. Though there are many, I would like to briefly discuss four of them.

The first obstacle concerns being honest about any past or current hurts. If we have been wounded in any intimate relationship, especially in marriage, we will need to get inner healing so as to not bring those wounds into our relationship with Jesus. (The same parallel is true for wounds incurred by our natural father or mother interrupting the connection to our Heavenly Father.) Past scars from a spouse or loved one that are unresolved will create roadblocks in our heart while trying to understand more about Jesus being our eternal spouse.

If the thought of a spouse or lover equals pain because of past hurts, then how can we think of knowing Jesus in the same way without flinching a little bit on the inside. If there are any feelings of anger, fear or anxiety connected to the past that hasn't been healed, this will transpose itself onto God. It's just the way things work, hence the need to start the conversation with Jesus (and others) about getting our wounds healed up in order to grow closer to Him. If we don't, then it's easy to start seeing God through old wounds. The enemy of our soul fans the flames of these wounds by equating the image of a spouse with a negative, critical taskmaster, someone who is impossible to please. Who would want to grow closer to that? Depending on the pain involved, this can distort our view of "God is our husband" into "God is our master" —and we are back to square one.

Please know that God only has the best and purest of intentions when using this term. In the Hebrew language, the word "husband" expresses love, affection, and sweetness. This is the highest metaphor and the strongest language God could use. Think about this: out of all the words in the dictionary, or better said, out of all the words in the universe, God chose this one word to describe Christ's ultimate connection in our lives: husband. Amazing!

~

Another obstacle to be aware of is connected to the last, but comes from a different direction. Even if we don't struggle with past wounds, for some reason we still feel safer and more comfortable viewing God as our master and with us being His lowly servant. In this scenario, we tend to pray from this lowly servant perspective, "God, just tell me what to do and I'll do it. All I want is to obey your words. Nothing more, nothing less." This keeps everything simple and orderly, unlike intimacy, which can be very messy and uncertain at times.

The problem is that even when we try to spin the master/servant relationship in a positive light, there will always be a distant, cold feel to our relationship; there will be a lack of partnership and closeness. Though this approach may seem spiritual, it will **never** take the place of marriage nor create the bond your Creator wants to have with you— forever! Don't be fooled by the religious feeling this deception creates.

~

The third obstacle is a cousin to the last one: it's the problem of shame. Because of our failures, and we all have them, the enemy of our soul loves to whisper in our ears how mad and disappointed God is with us. And if we believe this lie, the last thing we can imagine is that He wants to be close to us. Instead, we settle for what seems appropriate for our condition, and that is a lowly servant, which is a safe place for us to hide. We put ourselves in a spiritual jail, keeping intimacy at arm's length.

In our shame and disappointment, our heart inadvertently start saying things like, "I've let you down—again. Please, keep your distance. I don't deserve to be any closer." Painstaking guilt leads us to repeat the prodigal son's words in Luke, saying, *"I am no longer worthy to be called your son. Make me like one of your hired servants"* (Luke 15:19 NKJV).

Any position higher than a servant would seem too brash, too close, even scandalous. Shame and true friendship never go together, like oil and water. But that's why the good news is the good news! That's why His grace is so amazing! He is able to deliver you from shame, restoring you to your true identity!

❧

The last obstacle I would like to address concerns biblical metaphors, their strengths and weaknesses. Metaphors are an important tool to help communicate spiritual truths. They can help our minds make the connection between natural realities and spiritual truths. For example, when we refer to God as our "rock," we might picture His unshakeable strength in the midst of a storm. While this is a great allegory, especially in times of trouble, it is also impersonal. Typically, we don't draw close to a rock and tell it our deepest secrets. There is no intimacy with a stone!

Unfortunately, people often put the words "husband" and "bride," the most intimate terms God could use, in the same category as a stone; it's just poetic language, a metaphor. But I want us to be careful that when we talk about Jesus being a husband to us, we don't catalog this in our minds as just another parable or a biblical trivia answer instead of a living reality.

What complicates this challenge even more is when I hear these terms thrown around in a haphazard way by teachers and preachers, making it sound like super-spiritual jargon or a mystical illusion only for the super-spiritual. This muddies the water when we don't keep this language as a practical, living reality in our spiritual walk.

The truth of the matter is this: Jesus' desire is to be as

close to us as a good husband is to his wife, plain and simple. He really wants a bride! This is not some poetic allusion, but a reality He died for. Be aware of this subtle trap; don't take this one lightly because there is an encounter waiting for you on the other side of this "metaphor."

As you dig into the treasure chest of Hosea 2:16, my prayer is that all of these obstacles will turn into stepping stones towards a profound change in your spiritual life!

$\sim$

"For this reason a man will leave his father and mother and be united to his wife, and the two will become one flesh." **This is a profound mystery—but I am talking about Christ and the church.** (Ephesians 5:31–32 NIV, emphasis added)

Who is Jesus to you? When no one is around, the lights are off, and your eyes are closed, who do you see? Who do you hear? Your husband or your master?

As we wrestle with these questions, we need to remember that discovering Jesus as our husband is a *"profound mystery."* You cannot just read a verse in the Bible and declare the mystery solved. Proverbs 25:2 says, *"It is the glory of God to conceal a matter, but the glory of kings is to **search out a matter**"* (NKJV, emphasis added). God is excited to reveal the depths of this mystery to those whose hearts are hungry for more. This is a mystery He wants you to search out and discover.

Do you want to encounter the truth of Hosea 2:16? Then start the search!

7

HOW HUNGRY ARE YOU?

Blessed are those who hunger and thirst for righteousness, for they shall be satisfied.
—Matthew 5:6 NASB

Hunger can change the course of a life. It disrupts the normal way of living. If you pay attention to your hunger pains, they can cause the usual things in life to taste like desert sand. You begin to realize that normal life doesn't quench the deep thirst of the soul. This helps to create a knowing deep inside that there must be more.

When I first started to experience hunger for a deeper relationship with Jesus, my spiritual life changed—and got a little confusing at times. I wanted more of Jesus, but I didn't really want to give up or change anything in my day-to-day life to get more. At times, I felt spiritually stuck; wanting more but not sure what to do. But the thought of staying trapped in my empty condition motivated me to ask the Lord for help. I was tired of feeling like I was going nowhere in my walk with Christ.

One day while reading the Bible, Matthew 5:6 popped out at me in an unusual way, especially the last part of the verse: *"for they shall be satisfied"* (NASB). Up to this point in my life, I'm not sure I had ever experienced something I could call "being satisfied." Maybe I would feel that sense for a minute or two while praying or during a good church service, but definitely nothing prolonged. Most everything in life was actually the opposite of being satisfied. My curiosity was piqued. Yet, I was a little worried as well; was this just another spiritual carrot on a stick, another unreachable promise in the Bible—or was this something real and tangible?

> *I was tired of feeling like I was going nowhere in my walk with Christ.*

As I looked at this verse a little closer, I realized that being satisfied was possible but I had to walk through the doorway of hunger and thirst to get it. That made me nervous—what does hunger really mean? I knew that Jesus is safe and only has good intentions for me; if He promised that I would be blessed with satisfaction by going through this door, I had to try. I was so bored and dry inside, I had nothing to lose. But I also knew myself well enough to know that I couldn't just conjure hunger up out of nowhere on my own, so I started to ask for it. At first, this felt awkward and uncomfortable, and even scary at times; but after a while, new life began to awaken inside.

I soon discovered that Jesus loves to answer these kinds of prayers. He loves to draw us closer and to satisfy us in a way that's not humanly possible. Little by little, I could sense something was changing inside. Tiny spiritual hunger pains started to rumble around in my heart, and it was good. I felt my spirit growing.

When I first started to feel stirrings of hunger for a deeper walk, it caused me to reevaluate my priorities. Some things were going to have to change if I really wanted to make room for more of His presence. At times, I could sense the Holy Spirit nudge me about certain excesses that were taking up too much time and energy. I was worried at first that it would be hard to change. Thankfully, as I leaned into His amazing grace, these changes were actually easier than expected. To be frank, a lot of the things that use to be really important started to bore me anyway. Like I've mentioned before, Jesus really does help make these changes easier than we think, if we learn to lean into Him (See Matt. 11:28-30).

Slowly but surely, I gained the courage to live a different lifestyle to pursue Jesus more wholeheartedly. I didn't care what other people thought about my journey as much. I wanted life. I wanted more of Him, no matter what. Hunger changed the course of my life.

The beginning of the journey toward deeper intimacy with Christ comes down to one penetrating question: *How hungry are you?* I know from personal experience that this question is a game changer. And if you are brave enough to at least take a small step through this doorway, your life will be changed.

∾

Blessed are those who hunger and thirst for righteousness, for they shall be satisfied. (Matthew 5:6 NASB)

As I studied and meditated on this foundational passage, I discovered some truths that helped me understand this verse better. Let me briefly share a couple of these thoughts.

The first thing that caught my attention was the phrase "for righteousness." To be honest, this language bothered me. I was starting to find a little freedom from religion while discovering this new intimacy with Jesus, and these words seemed to be going back down the religious path. I would read this thinking that the pressure is back on my shoulders—I had to hunger and thirst for better actions; I had to try to behave in a more spiritual way. In other words, better behavior equaled better righteousness. This is one of the main foundations of religion, not the gospel.

Thankfully, I finally realized that to be hungry "for righteousness" wasn't about my actions: it was about Jesus. Please catch this! All I needed to be hungry for was Him. Let me explain.

According to Bible, Jesus is our righteousness, through faith in Him (1 Cor. 1:30; Phil. 3:9). Striving after good works is not righteousness. This is great news and changes everything! It redirects the focus of the heart. Furthermore, Jesus states in John 7:37, *"If anyone is thirsty, let him come to Me and drink"* (NASB). Jesus, not our good works, is the only thing that can satisfy our thirsty soul. Realizing this helps us to better understand what we are to hunger and thirst for.

So I simplified this verse a little, making it sound less religious by replacing the words "for righteousness" with the words "for Jesus." So, with this clarification in mind, another way to read Matthew 5:6 is: "Blessed are those who hunger and thirst for Me (Jesus), because I will completely satisfy them."

Another observation is this: it is Jesus who satisfies us, not ourselves. This may seem obvious, but how many times do we act as though it isn't? It is crucial to realize that we can never satisfy ourselves—only Jesus can. We cause ourselves much pain when we try to fill emptiness ourselves. We do this in various ways, from trying to serve God more to indulging ourselves with too much food or TV. We take over for Christ more than we are aware of, trying to fill our inner longings without realizing that it just doesn't work. It's important to ask the Lord to shine a light on these areas, inviting Him to come and satisfy.

Let's move on. If Jesus is to be the object of our hunger, and He is the only one who can satisfy us, then what is our part? Simply, to be hungry for Him. Jesus says that He blesses those who are hungry. Sounds easy, doesn't it? But if this is true, then it's critical to ask: *What is hunger? What does hunger mean to me? How does it impact my life?*

The problem with trying to define hunger is that we, in the western world, very seldom go hungry. Our concept of hunger is when we miss eating our Twinkies in between meals or when we skip a midnight snack. That's our paradigm of hunger. We have a very limited understanding of what this means.

The word "hunger" in the original Greek language of the New Testament means "to suffer, to be needy, to seek with eager desire." The picture of hunger is of someone who is starving out in the middle of the desert, searching desperately for food and water. Jesus was painting a graphic picture with His words. It would be easy to read over these words through a western lens with little thought, but Jesus' audience lived in a different culture and context—a desert region—where his hearers were well-acquainted with hunger. They didn't have to stretch their imagination to picture what this really meant.

This type of hunger sounds painful to me. I don't like to be needy. I don't like to suffer want. No one taught me that being desperate was a good thing. Being stuffed and filled was always the goal. Little did I realize that Jesus sometimes uses hunger pains to draw us into new areas of friendship. Fortunately, He loves to satisfy and heal those pains; He doesn't leave us stuck.

∾

With this definition of hunger in mind, let me reword Matthew 5:6 once again: "Blessed are those who painfully feel their want of Me, to the point of eagerly seeking Me at all cost. For in that place of hunger, I will completely satisfy them."

The phrase "to the point of eagerly seeking Me at all cost" is the purpose of hunger. If you are not hungry to the point of eagerly seeking Jesus at all cost, then the hunger is in vain— it's meaningless. Hunger pains must take us somewhere transformative to be effective. They were never meant just to make us miserable. It is not a holy or honorable thing to be stuck in the desert with no hope of being satisfied. (That sounds like hell on earth to me.) We were created to be satisfied, but only by Jesus.

Hunger is the fuel of seeking. Hunger is what opens the door to deeper levels of friendship and intimacy with Christ. Hunger is what drives us to want to know Him more. The beginning of this journey to develop a deep and rich friendship with Jesus is far simpler than most people make it. We don't need some big spiritual experience to start, although, if it does happen, that's great. We also don't need some big-name pastor or evangelist to pray for us to begin this journey.

The first step is to simply ask Jesus to instill in us a hunger for more of Him. This is so simple, yet foundational. Ask, seek, and knock (Luke 11:9-10) for life-changing hunger.

Just know this: being hungry is a free gift Christ will give you if you want it. I guarantee it! This is good news! But also know—it will cost you everything. Hunger is a divine paradox: it's free, but

There is a divine promise - you will be satisfied!

costly. This God-given hunger will change the course of your life, if you let it. You will never be the same. There is a divine blessing on hunger. Likewise, there is a divine promise—you will be satisfied! This makes the cost worth it.

Passion knows no logic. Logic would have said to Mary of the alabaster box (Matt. 26:6–13), "Don't do this. You can't afford it." But passion said, "I can't afford not to."[1]

So the question before you is this: **How hungry are you?**

8

___

JUNK FOOD AND TREADMILLS

On this journey toward more intimacy, there are what I call the "in-between times" of life, or times of delay. These are seasons when we are hungry for more of God but we don't sense that He is near. We start strong, but then when nothing happens like we expected, the anticipation wears off. Pursuing Jesus with real excitement gives way to disappointment. We feel let down and frustrated, causing us to enter these dry, desolate in-between times.

This can be a dangerous place to be because we are open to attacks from the enemy of our soul. For example, in Exodus 32:1, when God delayed Moses from coming down from Mount Sinai, the Israelites wanted something they could see, touch, and feel, just like we do at times. They wanted something to replace Moses' presence. So they cried out to Aaron, "Where is Moses? We can't see him. Make us something to replace him. Make us an idol; something we can put our hands on, something we can touch, feel and even control" (my translation). If you know the story, Aaron made a golden calf for the people to worship, which obviously did not sit well with the Lord.

It's during these in-between times, or the delays of life, when we can lose sight of the process and turn to other things to satisfy us. This is where satan can set all sorts of booby traps to keep us from the treasure of learning how to sense His still small voice. Let's look briefly at just two of these traps.

Trap number one is "junk food." Once again, raw hunger pain is the fuel of seeking. We seek Him because we are hungry for Him (at least at the beginning; as we mature, we keep seeking based on having a deeper friendship). Instead of letting the hunger drive us closer to Christ, we tend to satisfy those hunger twinges by overeating junk food. We ease those pains with a little of this and a little of that in life. And before you know it, our hearts are too full with no hunger left for Him.

It's the same principle in the natural. One of my favorite meals is a steak dinner. If I eat ten candy bars right before the meal, no matter how much I love steak, I will not be hungry for the main course. It's just a fact of life. Please note that the "candy bars" of life are not the problem. The problem is when they become the meal.

Here is a question that we must wrestle with: Are our personal lives so full of the junk food of life that we no longer have any hunger left for Him? Instead of letting hunger pains drive us deeper in our walk with Christ, do we dull these pains with too much "snack food?"

Sometimes in my own life, it has been easy for me to get distracted during the painful times of delay, to coast away from Him by diving deeper into my hobbies or work. Even though I have had the best of intentions, at times I have turned to books, TV, and even shopping to dull my hunger pains. Please hear me: these things are not wrong in and of themselves; it's when we run to these things to satisfy our inner longings or to cover up pain that they become harmful.

During these times, my spiritual life can look like a squirrel caught in a cage, running in circles, going nowhere. I just keep busy doing something, anything to keep me distracted from the ache inside. Thankfully, Holy Spirit's gentle voice is always there to expose the emptiness of what I am doing and how I am feeling, asking probing questions like: "Are you satisfied yet? Are you tired? Are you ready for life? How hungry are you?"

~

Trying to quench our hunger pains in an unhealthy way is like Matthew 24:37–39, where Jesus proclaimed:

> *"For the coming of the Son of Man will be just like the days of Noah. For as in those days which were before the flood they were eating and drinking, they were marrying and giving in marriage, until the day that Noah entered the ark, and they did not understand until the flood came and took them all away; so shall the coming of the Son of Man be."* (NASB)

People in Noah's day, like our own, were absorbed in everyday life. Obviously, it was not wrong to eat, drink, or marry, but such activities consumed them at the expense of having a love affair with their Creator. They were passionate about the *secondary* things in life, as though they were the *primary* things in life. *Legitimate*, God-ordained activities became *illegitimate*. In other words, the first commandment had lost its first place. Loving God was not first in their lives. The good news for us is that, as followers of Christ, we can ask the Holy Spirit to show us our priorities and help us rearrange them. He does not leave us alone on this journey.

If asked, I believe that most Christians would say that they want a closer walk with Jesus. But the problem is that *wanting* a closer walk is different from being *hungry* for one. Wanting something is far different from pursuing something. I can want to be a football or basketball player but not ever pursue being one. To be an athlete, you give up the junk food voluntarily. Not because you have to or are being manipulated, but because you want to. There is this inner desire to be the best at your sport. You start to eat right and exercise; you put time and energy into it—not because someone manipulated you into doing it or put a guilt trip on you. You did it because you have this inner passion and desire to be a great player.

Similarly, this journey of friendship with Jesus is driven by desire. It's driven by hunger! It's not driven by command or coercion or shame. A healthy romance is never fueled by such things but by desire, passion, and hunger. So the question is: how hungry are you?

Friendship with Jesus is driven by desire

❧

The second trap is equally dangerous and even more subtle. This trap lures us to step onto the treadmill of life called "doing more." When I was growing up, our pastor would bring in traveling speakers to teach the congregation. Some of them had attitudes like hired guns from the Old West—they were going to straighten us all out, one way or another. It felt like they were brought in to beat us up to make us better Christians.

Their message always seemed to have the same theme: try harder and do more; do this and don't do that; and most importantly, please do it the right way. As I got older, the common wisdom in the Christian culture was more of the same: if you want a closer walk with Jesus, try harder by doing more: pray more, read the Bible more, give more money—more, more, more.

Using a few Bible verses out of context, these sermons on doing "more" really seemed hard to argue with because they sounded so right. I would hear things like, "If you would read your Bible more consistently, your problem will work itself out just fine," or "If you would pray more every day, you wouldn't be struggling with those issues."

After I burned myself out trying to fulfill all these expectations, I asked myself: *When do I know that I've done enough? If I am praying ten minutes a day, will God love me more if I increase it to twenty minutes? Or what is the secret amount of Bible reading to really make God happy? If I'm reading two chapters a day, do I need to double it to four? Or if I'm extra spiritual, do I go for eight chapters?*

So during these high-powered church services, I would make really big commitments to God: I'm going to pray six hours and read twenty-four chapters of the Bible every single day! Then I would go for it in a big way. I would set the alarm clock earlier than normal and try to hit it hard—at least for a few minutes, until I would doze back off to sleep. Does this sound familiar?

Shortly thereafter, when I couldn't live up to those commitments, condemnation and shame would wash over me. I would feel like a second-class person in my walk with Christ. I could never measure up to some unreachable standard that loomed before me. A closer walk with Jesus always seemed just beyond my grasp, even though others around me looked to be doing just fine.

Inevitably, the pain of these failures caused me to turn back to the junk-food of life. I would try even harder to pull life from my job, hobbies, and entertainment to fill up the emptiness in my heart—at least until the next guest speaker came along. Then the cycle would start all over again.

For most of my early adult years, I felt stuck between these traps—the emptiness of junk food and the treadmill of doing more. This up-and-down cycle was a normal way of life for me. I was confused and tormented, trying to find peace in my Christian walk, but to no avail. The cycle would just keep repeating itself. After feeling down for a while, I would make new commitments and think, *I'm going to try even harder and be more devoted.* I would feel some sense of accomplishment for a short time and think, *Jesus loves me more now.* Then after a bad week or month, I would feel ashamed and condemned all over again, which caused me to go back even harder into my work, hobbies, or entertainment—anything to cover up the pain of another failure.

I never felt like I could enter into this rest.

Later, the Holy Spirit would knock on my door again, wooing me closer to His heart. His nudges were strong, but my responses to them were not. Because I didn't understand His true amazing grace for intimacy, I would start the cycle all over again, saying: "Ok Lord, I'm going to try even harder this time, and I won't let you down!" I would have a good month and pat myself on the back, then a bad month, falling off the wagon once again. What a defeated and tormented life I was leading! Does this sound familiar?

I read in the Gospels where Jesus promised us rest, but wondered, *Is this real? Is it true?* I never felt like I could enter into this rest. It seemed so distant and unreachable. **How does one find this true rest?**

9

WILL I WHAT?

There is an old saying: "Good is the enemy of best." I have a new saying: "More is the enemy of all." Trying to do more for God is the enemy of giving all to Him. What do I mean by giving all?

Believe it or not, Jesus is not asking us: "Will you pray more?" "Will you read the Bible more?" "Will you give more?" "Will you go to church more?" His question is not "Will you do more, more, more?" That's a religious spirit trying to keep you trapped, spinning your spiritual wheels, going nowhere.

Instead, Jesus' question to us today is this: **"Will you marry Me?"**

Can you let this bold question sink in? "Will you marry Me?" You might be thinking, *Will I WHAT? Isn't that a little forward? I hardly know you.* I know this may seem difficult, but try to imagine Jesus standing before you, face to face, asking one simple question: "Will *you* marry Me?" Saying "Yes" to this question is the true essence of giving all.

I know this is a shocking question, even a strange one at

first—especially for men. From one man to another, remember that this is not about letting go of your man card, per se. This is not about any male/female role playing. Please catch this: it's about being invited into a position of closeness. It's about understanding His desire for closeness—thus discovering the real reason for creation! (If you can truly digest this last statement, you will be amazed at how your view of life will change.)

If you are willing to push past all the uncomfortableness of this brash question—if you can push past all of your guilt and shame—if you can push past all the past religious barriers —if you are willing to risk it all and say, "I do" to the King of kings and the Lord of lords, you will open the door to a deep friendship that will change your life forever. Slowly, you will quit trying to give Him more by working harder. Instead, you will want to give Him *all*. This is where *true rest* is discovered! It's the rest of intimacy.

Religion always wants more, but is never satisfied with what you can give.

If you start saying yes to this question, you will slowly transition out of religion and into relationship, even though it may be hard and confusing at first. Religion always wants more, but is never satisfied with what you can give. It takes time to realize that Jesus doesn't operate that way. He looks for the yes in your heart and runs with that. That's all it takes to start this amazing friendship—a simple yes! He promises that this journey is not burdensome and hard; instead you will discover rest for you soul (Matt. 11:28-30). This is the opposite of the struggle that is required to do more.

Jesus is after your heart, not just your actions, because when He has your heart, your actions will naturally follow.

Just like in a physical marriage, as you mature in love, your service starts to flow more naturally, joyfully, and wholeheartedly towards the object of your love. This quote says it best: "A lover will out-work a worker." For example, a business owner will love and care for his company more than a hired hand will. In the kingdom of God, if you are just a hired hand, you will only do what is required. On the other hand, if you are a lover of God, you will give your all—your life— for the One you love.

~

The question at hand is a proposal from the One who loves you more than anyone else. It is an invitation to life and freedom. But no one can force you to say yes to Him. You must want it, or it will never happen. The journey toward intimacy is one of desire, not command. When I proposed marriage to my wife, I was not just looking for her to give me the right answer or for her to feel manipulated to say yes to me out of obligation or fear. Instead, I was looking for her eager desire behind the right answer, the excitement to spend the rest of our lives together.

Let me illustrate this a little further with a confrontation Jesus had with those who felt obligated to do the right thing. In Matthew 9:14, John the Baptist's disciples came to Jesus asking a simple question: *"How is it that we and the Pharisees fast, but your disciples do not fast?"* (NIV) At first glance, this might seem like an innocent question, but in truth, it was a loaded one. What they were really asking was this: "Hey Jesus, what's the deal? We are doing all these activities, obeying all the commandments, even doing all the right fasts; but your guys are not. What's going on here?"

In verses 15–17, Jesus answers them:

How can the guests of the bridegroom mourn while he is with them? The time will come when the bridegroom will be taken from them; then they will fast. No one sews a patch of unshrunk cloth on an old garment, for the patch will pull away from the garment, making the tear worse. Neither do men pour new wine into old wineskins. If they do, the skins will burst, the wine will run out and the wineskins will be ruined. No, they pour new wine into new wineskins, and both are preserved. (NIV)

There are a lot of verses here, but let me rephrase them—here is the heart of Jesus' words:

Others fast, pray, read their Bibles, go to church, and even give money out of command, obligation, and religious duty; it's the "right" thing to do. But this journey toward friendship with Me—the Bridegroom—is not done by command or obligation or religious duty. It is driven by desire. And there will be those who understand who I am, their Bridegroom, the Lover of their souls; they will pursue Me—not because they have to, not because they are pressured or manipulated to, but because they *want to* out of hunger and thirst for Me. When I am gone, they will fast (or mourn) for more of me; they will long for Me; they will be desperate for Me, their Bridegroom and King.

And when they enter into this pursuit, the new wine of friendship and intimacy with Me will start to flow into their lives. Their old wineskins—their old ways of living—will not be able to contain this new wine anymore. It will require new wineskins—new lifestyle changes—to contain this. The way they spend their time will change. The way they spend their money will change. The way they spend their energy and thought life will change. Not because they *have to*—but because they *want to.*

These people will not be manipulated anymore by someone pointing a condemning finger at them. This is not legalism, but a love affair with Me, the King of kings. Instead of struggling to pray ten minutes a week, their prayer life will take on new dynamics; it will start to flow without ceasing. Instead of reading the Bible out of duty and obligation, they will be consumed by their desire to go deeper into our relationship. Life will never be the same.

With this declaration, Jesus pushed the reset button to the old church system. Following Him wasn't going to be out of religious duty, but out of intimacy.

~

Are you ready for the new wine of intimacy with Christ? I am. I've tasted a little and I want more. Intimacy is addicting. I also know that I need His amazing grace for a new wine skin to hold more of His presence; otherwise, I will fall back into doing more and trying harder. The great thing is that God gives grace for a lifestyle change to those who persistently ask, seek, and knock for it. Jesus loves to answer the cry for more of Him.

The good news of the Gospel is this: **Jesus Christ desires you like no other.** If you get nothing else out of this book, please get this: He desires you like no other!

Jesus Christ desires you like no other

Coming to Jesus is not just about saying some magical prayer and keeping a set of rules to get into heaven someday. It's about stepping into a new life and new lifestyle with the Creator of the universe.

Jesus is passionate for you! He is so passionate that He is asking each and every one of us this life-changing question:

"Will you marry Me?"

10

THE CHASE IS ON

One day Rabbi Barukh's grandson Yehiel was playing hide-and-seek with another boy. He hid himself well and waited for his playmate to find him. After twenty minutes, he peeked out of his secret hiding place, saw no one, and pulled his head back inside. After waiting a very long time, he came out of his hiding place, but the other boy was nowhere to be seen. Then Yehiel realized that his playmate had not looked for him from the very beginning. Crying, he ran to his grandfather and complained of his faithless friend.
Tears brimmed in Rabbi Barukh's eyes as he realized:
God says the same thing: **I hide but no one wants to seek me.**
— Brennan Manning, Signature of Jesus[1]

I was in college the first time I saw my future wife, and I was hooked! Immediately, I had to find out who she was, what classes she was in, and what she liked. Wherever she went, I wanted to go. Whatever she was doing, I wanted to participate. Whatever else I was involved in I dropped instantly. My priorities changed. The chase had begun. Later, the chase had a great ending—we married! Then a new chase began—staying married for over thirty years to an amazing person!

God loves to be chased. He loves to be pursued. The fire of romance burns brighter when the chase is on. It takes *seeking* to produce *finding*. Christ, who pursues us as His cherished bride, wants to be pursued as well. He wants us to have the same attitude as the bride did in the Song of Solomon when she cries out, *"I must seek him whom my soul loves"* (Song 3:2 NASB). What a determined cry of the heart! Shortly after, she states, *"When I found him whom my soul loves; I held on to him and would not let him go"* (Song 3:4 NASB).

> *Some spiritual treasures will never be found by accident, but only by looking for them*

I want this same passion and focus in my life. The fruit of seeking is finding more and more of Him, which truly satisfies the soul. This spiritual satisfaction makes me want to hold onto what I've found and not let go. God reserves depths of intimacy for those who seek for it with this same tenacity and zeal, for those who *"press on to know the* LORD*"* (Hosea 6:3 NASB). In other words, some spiritual treasures will never be found by accident, but only by looking for them.

Years ago, when the Lord started to awaken my heart to the possibility of a deeper walk, He highlighted one word to me over and over in the Bible: *seek*. What a simple word with so much behind it. God loves a seeking heart. This word is the launching pad to more of God.

Deuteronomy 4:29 encapsulates the context of this word best: *"But from there you will **seek** the LORD your God, and you will find Him **if you search** for Him with all your heart and all your soul"* (NASB, emphasis added). The way to finding more of God is clearly spelled out: seeking will produce finding.

There are two key Hebrew words used in this verse: "seek" (*baqash*) and "search" (*darash*), both with parallel meanings. The word "seek" is "often used to describe the 'seeking of' the Lord in the sense of entering a **covenantal relationship** with Him."[2] Are you starting to see the pattern with God's heart toward having a covenantal (i.e., marriage) relationship with us? Jesus is pursuing us for marriage and wants an equally-yoked bride who pursues Him back.

∾

The Bible has several words for the act of seeking God (darash, bakkesh, shahar). In some passages, these words are used in the sense of inquiring after His will and precepts (Psalms 119:45, 94, 155). Yet, in other passages these words mean more than the act of asking a question, the aim of which is to elicit information. **It means addressing oneself directly to God with the aim of getting close to Him; it involves a desire for experience rather than a search for information. . . . Indeed, to pray does not only mean to seek help; it also means to seek Him.**
—Abraham Heschel, *God in Search of Man* [3]

The primary meaning of these Hebrew words is "to seek with care . . . to seek [with a demand], to demand, to require."[4] The phrase "to seek [with a demand], to demand, to require" captures something about the nature of intimacy with God that I would like to point out. This may seem awkward and too forward, but God is telling us to demand and require more of Him. He wants pursuit. He loves someone trying to capture more.

God is giving us permission, even daring us, to come after Him in a unique, wholehearted way

I know that this might be hard to let in and may sound scary—demanding more of God—but this is what He wants. God is giving us permission, even daring us, to come after Him in a unique, wholehearted way. To seek "with a demand" is having an attitude where you can't and won't live without more of Him. There is a passion that burns deep inside to pursue Him *"with all your heart and all your soul."*

This intensity is paralleled in Isaiah 55:6 which says: *"Seek, inquire for, and require the LORD while He may be found [claiming Him by necessity and by right]; call upon Him while He is near"* (AMP, emphasis added). *"Claiming Him by necessity"* captures the heart of "demanding" more of God. When you come to the end of yourself and realize that the one true need, the one true desire of your life is only found in the romance of the gospel, you won't have any trouble understanding what these passages mean.

～

The pivotal word in Deuteronomy 4:29 is "if" (*"you will find Him if you search for Him,"* emphasis added). Seeking or going after something does not happen by accident—it is a choice. There are certain theologies and teachers of the Bible who seem to ignore this important word "if." They imply that

God dictates everything in the world, including our closeness to Him, leaving no room for choices or responsibilities.

Some people live as though spiritual growth is all up to God, but this is not true. Their prevailing wisdom says, "If it's meant to be, it will happen." This sad logic prevents many from experiencing more intimacy in their lives. Think about how many marriages and friendships would have never happened with this kind of thinking. Ignoring God's invitation to seek Him leads to apathy and a boring religious life.

Still others think that spiritual growth is all up to them. They live with the pressure that they must make all growth and progress happen. This is not true either. As with most things, there is a balance. The journey toward more intimacy is not all up to us; it is a co-laboring effort. It is a spiritual paradox that takes 100 percent God and 100 percent us. It is God's amazing grace and our surrender to His grace.

In the book of Colossians, Paul adds another layer to this tension: *"And for this purpose also **I labor**, striving according to **His power**, which mightily works within me"* (Col. 1:29 NASB, emphasis added). You do have to labor, but you also have His power. Abraham Heschel beautifully explains the balance this way: "Without God's aid, man cannot find Him. Without man's seeking, His aid is not granted."[5]

Another verse is Psalm 63:8, which states, *"My whole being **follows hard** after You and clings closely to You; Your right hand **upholds** me"* (AMP, emphasis added). We *"follow hard"* after God while He *"upholds"* us in our pursuit. It takes two to make a marriage work. The Hebrew word for the phrases *"follows hard"* and *"clings closely"* is *dabaq,* which means to "cling or adhere; figuratively, **to catch by pursuit**."[6]

We "catch" more of God by pursuing Him, which is one of the foundations of all love affairs. I would have never caught my wife without first pursuing her. Whatever you love is what you will pursue wholeheartedly and give your life for. It is interesting that Genesis 2:24 uses this exact same Hebrew word (*dabaq*) to describe a man being "joined" (*dabaq*) to his wife to become one in marriage.

So what are the results of seeking? There are many listed in the Bible. Here are just a few:

- *Let the heart of those who seek the LORD* **be glad.** (1 Chronicles 16:10 NASB, emphasis added)
- *If you seek Him, He will let you* **find Him.** (1 Chronicles 28:9 NASB, emphasis added)
- *But they who seek the LORD shall* **not be in want** *of any good thing.* (Psalm 34:10 NASB, emphasis added)
- **Blessed** *are those who keep His testimonies, Who seek Him with the whole heart!* (Psalm 119:2 NKJV, emphasis added)
- *I love those who love me; And those who diligently seek me* **will find** *me.* (Proverbs 8:17 NASB, emphasis added)
- *But those who wait (***to look eagerly for***[7]) on the LORD shall* **renew their strength***; They shall mount up with wings like eagles, They shall run and not be weary, They shall walk and not faint.* (Isaiah 40:31 NKJV, emphasis added)
- *The LORD* **is good** *to those who wait for Him, To the person who seeks Him.* (Lamentations 3:25 NASB, emphasis added)
- *Blessed are those who hunger and thirst for righteousness, for they shall* **be satisfied***.* (Matthew 5:6 NASB, emphasis added)

- *Draw near to God and He will **draw near** to you.*
(James 4:8 NASB, emphasis added)

❧

Once again, the Lord loves to be chased. He loves a seeking heart. Jesus is drawn to those who want more of Him—who even *demand* more of Him. His heart is captured by our pursuit. Likewise, in an amazing way, our pursuit opens our hearts to be captured by Him as well.

Seek Him with a heart that won't be denied, and discover what happens.

❧

*The prophets' presentation of the covenant as a marriage union is not ... to equate it with a domestic bond. Nor is it a metaphorical way of explaining Yahweh's relationship with Israel. The prophets seized upon the essence of the covenant— undivided, reciprocal love—and saw Yahweh's union with Israel for what it really was, **a marriage union**....*

*The meaning and culmination of all salvation history may thus be seen as the realization of a marriage covenant in which God takes the initiative, and man, **as responding bride, opens himself to God and presses on toward Him with the longing cry: Come.***[8]

11

COVENANT OF LOVE

We (need to) experience the forgiveness of Jesus not as the reprieve of a judge, but the embrace of a lover. [1]

~

*For centuries prior to our Modern Era, the church viewed the gospel as a Romance.... But our rationalistic approach to life, which has dominated Western culture for hundreds of years, has stripped us of that, leaving a faith that is barely more than mere fact-telling. Modern evangelicalism reads like an IRS 1040 form: It's true, all the data is there, **but it doesn't take your breath away***.*
— *Brent Curtis and John Eldredge, The Sacred Romance* [2]

W hen I first started to study about Christ wanting to be married to us, I was overwhelmed with the number of direct and indirect Bible references surrounding this topic. Some are partial verses but others are complete passages and chapters devoted to this topic. I also discovered that even the meanings of some of the key Hebrew words in the Bible (i.e., "love," "to know" and "lovingkindness") have strong marital overtones. With these being some of the most important words in the Bible, this really impacted me.

Growing up in the church, I don't remember being taught anything about covenantal love. Of course, there were passing references to it, but nothing of any depth concerning my day-to-day walk with Him. And what was taught seemed to be referencing something mystical or mysterious, but nothing practical for present reality. Thankfully, today there are more teachers in the body of Christ that are starting to give us a better understanding on this important topic.

In this chapter, I want to give a brief overview of a few passages of Scripture that give some insight into God's feelings and desires for us. It would take volumes to be comprehensive, but hopefully, this will kick-start your search. (Because I have sprinkled many New Testament verses throughout the entire book, I will mostly list a few Old Testament examples here for the sake of brevity.)

There are three key marriages mentioned in the Bible that help shape our understanding of God's desire for a covenantal relationship with the human race. According to Jewish tradition, the first wedding is when God married Adam and Eve in the garden: *"Therefore a man shall leave his father and mother and be joined to his wife, and they shall become one flesh"* (Gen. 2:24 NKJV). Interestingly, this special uniting of two people to become one is also a picture of the third wedding—our wedding with Christ—which I will cover in the next chapter.

From the beginning, marriage has been a part of humanity's physical and spiritual DNA—it's the blueprint of our design. The marriage vows from Genesis 2:24 tell the story of what Jesus wanted with us from the very beginning of time: to be *one* with us forever! (See Eph. 5:28–33.) We were created for love. We were never meant to be alone.

After the fall of Adam and Eve, the second wedding took place when God established a covenantal relationship with the nation of Israel at Mount Sinai (see Exod. 19 and 20) and described this union as a marriage. This event is

We were created for love. We were never meant to be alone.

when God gave the Israelites the Torah and the Ten Commandments, which Jewish commentaries consider part of their wedding covenant.

A thousand years after this event, God, speaking through Jeremiah, points back to this event at Mount Sinai and clarifies it as a bridal covenant, a marriage proposal: *"Go and cry in the ears of Jerusalem, saying, 'Thus says the LORD: I [earnestly] remember the kindness and devotion of your youth,* **your love after your betrothal [in Egypt] and marriage [at Sinai] when you followed Me** *in the wilderness, in a land not sown'"* (Jer. 2:2 AMP, emphasis added). The NIV Bible simplifies the key phrase: *"how* **as a bride you loved me** *and followed me through the desert."* Simply put, God married His bride, Israel, in the desert.

Another passage in Jeremiah also makes this case, but goes a step further by describing the new covenant (or new marriage proposal) that was to come with the Messiah:

"The time is coming," declares the LORD, "when I will make a new covenant with the house of Israel and with the house of

Judah. It will not be like the covenant I made with their forefathers when I took them by the hand to lead them out of Egypt, because they broke my covenant, **though I was a husband to them,** *" declares the* LORD. *"This is the covenant I will make with the house of Israel after that time," declares the* LORD. *"I will put my law in their minds and write it on their hearts.* **I will be their God, and they will be my people.** *"* (Jer. 31:31–33 NIV, emphasis added)

I included verse 33 as an example of one of the many "hidden" words or phrases that are marriage-related but aren't easily recognized as such. The phrase, *"I will be their God, and they will be my people,"* which is mentioned several times throughout the Old Testament (Jer. 24:7; 30:22; 31:1; 32:38; Ezek. 11:20; 37:27, and others), is a "legal formula taken from the sphere of marriage, as attested in various legal documents from the Ancient Near East."[3] Other sources clarify that this type of language was used in marriage ceremonies of that day. This phrase is equal to some of our current wedding vows when the bride and bridegroom say, "I, _____, take you, _____, to be my lawfully wedded (husband/wife), to have and to hold . . ."

When God said, *"I will be their God,"* He was declaring to His people, "I take you to be my lawfully wedded wife." In other words, "I do!" By repeating this phrase, God was reaffirming His heart's desire to have a covenantal (marriage) relationship with His people. Sadly, His bride, Israel, broke her vows many times, breaking His heart.

~

The believer is even more intimate with the Lord than with his or her spouse, for this is a union of spirit, and spirit always leads one more deeply into reality than does the flesh. The "cleaving to the Lord" of Deuteronomy 10:20 is now seen to be actualized through a joining of the believer's spirit with Christ. No more profound communion exists than that between the believer and the Lord. [4]

Sprinkled throughout the Old Testament are many references that reaffirm the marital relationship God had with his people. Unfortunately, many of them were negative. One such reference that was used is "playing the harlot" (committing adultery), which some of the Old Testament authors used without any qualification or explanation. They assumed their readers understood the relational dynamic between God and Israel as a known fact when using these terms. (For further study, here are just a few of the passages that refer to Israel being a harlot in their marriage relationship with God: Exod. 34:15-16; Deut. 31:16; Isa. 23:17; Jer. 2:20, 3; 5:7; 13:27; Ezek. 6:9; 16:6-63; 23; 43:7-9; Hosea 4:10–19; 6:10; 9:1; Nah. 3:4).

One of the more descriptive passages from this list is Ezekiel 16:30–32:

"How weak-willed you are," declares the Sovereign LORD, *"when you do all these things, acting like a brazen prostitute! When you built your mounds at the head of every street and made your lofty shrines in every public square, you were unlike a prostitute, because you scorned payment.* **You adulterous wife! You prefer strangers to your own husband!***"* (NIV, emphasis added)

Back to a more positive perspective, here are a few out of many passages where God identifies Himself as our husband:

- *"Return, faithless people," declares the* LORD, *"for I am your husband. I will choose you."* (Jer. 3:14 NIV, emphasis added)
- *"For your Maker is your husband—the* LORD *Almighty is his name."* (Isa. 54:5 NIV emphasis added)
- *"As a bridegroom rejoices over his bride, so will your God rejoice over you."* (Isa. 62:5 NIV, emphasis added)

∼

Another key word that describes God's heart is captured in Zechariah 8:2: *"This is what the* LORD *Almighty says: 'I am very jealous* (or *"zealous"* [NKJV]) *for Zion; I am burning with jealousy for her'"* (NIV, emphasis added). God's jealousy is an area of His personality that has been misunderstood and misrepresented. He is not an angry God who barely tolerates His creation. Likewise, He is not like the proverbial jealous husband who flies into a rage every time his wife does something he doesn't want her to do. In the Hebrew language, God's jealousy speaks of a righteous zeal and passion, sometimes with a holy anger, but never out of envy or resentment. J. I. Packer defines God's jealousy as a "zeal to protect a love-relationship, or to avenge it when broken."[5]

A sermon I once heard clarifies the intent of God's jealousy best:

Understand that the choice of this particular word ("jealous") in this text (Exod. 20:1–6, the wedding covenant) reveals to us something of the heart of God—the character of God, the true image of God—and how it is He has chosen to know us and how it is He has chosen to relate to us. Through this word, God says this to us about Himself, "I am not only your Creator, I am not only your Redeemer, your Deliverer, your Healer, your Provider—I want you to know that I am also your Lover!" Thus, the jealousy. This is where the word "jealous" comes from: a lover with very strong feelings about you.[6]

The great thing about God's jealousy is that it speaks of His passionate pursuit of us for friendship and intimacy. He is not distant or uncaring but full of zeal and passion. It should excite us that He wants an intimate relationship with us. We are always on His mind and heart. On the other hand, He won't share us with other lovers.

～

Lastly, the most explicit and revealing part in the Old Testament that looks at God's desire for a marriage relationship with Israel (and the church) is the Song of Songs (or Song of Solomon). To some, this is a very uncomfortable book, even a little scary—if not heretical. They cannot comprehend how it could be about Christ and us, His bride. Instead they try to make it a "safe" book by saying it is only about physical love between a man and a woman in the natural. But throughout Jewish history, it is known as the picture of a love affair between God and His bride. One Jewish author described it best:

This concept (of bride and groom symbols being used for God and Israel) found its grand culmination in one of the most beautiful poetic works of all time, King Solomon's Song of Songs. Though in external form it is a lyrical celebration of human love, Torah tradition reads the Song of Songs as a sublime metaphor of the spiritual marriage between God and Israel, a wedding which took place at the Revelation at Sinai. In Jewish tradition, the Song of Songs is a dialogue of love between Israel, the bride, and God, her beloved. God's divine love for His people is couched in the language of deep human emotion.

R. Akiva, the great Sage of the Mishnah, was emphatic about the transcendent spiritual significance of the Song of Songs. "All of the books of the Torah are holy," said R. Akiva, "but the Song of Songs is the 'Holy of Holies'; indeed, the entire world attained its supreme value on the day the Song of Songs was given to Israel." [7]

Never underestimate the glance of your eyes

The Song of Songs has many layers of meaning and insight. There is a lifetime of discoveries to be made in this amazing book, but one of my favorites is found in 4:9, where the bridegroom (Jesus) says: *"You have stolen my heart, my sister* (which means "spouse"), *my bride; you have stolen my heart with one glance of your eyes"* (NIV). The nugget of gold here is that it only takes a "glance" of your eyes (or your heart) to capture His heart! It's that easy! He never tries to make having a love affair complicated.

Never underestimate the glance of your eyes. We glance at Him by shifting our hearts toward Him in many ways, including worship, talking to Him (prayer), meditating on

His Word, etc. Your devotion to Him is more powerful (and easier) than you may think. Can you imagine "stealing" God's heart?

Please know this: **He is waiting to be captured by your love**.

12

CRAZY IN LOVE

When a person is in love, his beloved is the focus of his being. His entire consciousness is focused on his beloved to the exclusion of all else. Love enters the innermost recesses of the soul, and the deepest chambers of the heart. His mind is on his beloved day and night, in every waking moment, and in every dream. He only lives for the times that they can be together. Now, imagine a person having the same relationship toward God. Imagine him having the same passion toward God as the greatest passion that exists between man and woman.
— *Rabbi Aryeh Kaplan, Made in Heaven* [1]

The third key marriage or wedding in the Bible is represented by the New Covenant. This covenant represents the marriage between Christ and those who choose to follow Him, His church. This is the parallel wedding to the first one in the garden of Eden. The apostle Paul, in

Ephesians, re-interprets the first marriage covenant that is described in Genesis through the revelation of Jesus Christ:

> *"For this reason a man shall leave his father and mother and be joined to his wife, and the two shall become one flesh." **This is a great mystery, but I speak concerning Christ and the church.*** (Eph. 5:31–32 NKJV, emphasis added)

Paul explains that what happens in a physical marriage—two people becoming as one—is a symbol, an illustration of what Jesus desires to experience with us in our spiritual lives. Please let this truth stun you!

The first wedding in the garden of Eden was more than a natural event; it was a sign pointing toward a relationship between a Messiah and a redeemed people. The depth of intimacy that two people can experience in the physical world through romance and marriage is a mysterious and wonderful picture of the intimacy that can be experienced with Christ in our hearts. This is a great mystery worth exploring!

In 2 Corinthians 11, Paul also clarifies our position with Christ and the responsibility that comes with it. He states, *"For I am jealous for you with a godly jealousy; for **I betrothed you to one husband**, so that to Christ I might present you as a pure virgin. But I am afraid that, as the serpent deceived Eve by his craftiness, your minds will be led astray from the simplicity and purity of devotion to Christ"* (2 Cor. 11:2–3 NASU, emphasis added). I like how the *Today's English Version* states the key phrase: *"You are like a pure virgin **whom I have promised in marriage to one man only, Christ** himself."* Paul's greatest mission was to unite the church to Christ in marriage.

But Paul also warns us that it can be easy to lose this basic focus and *"be led astray from the simplicity* (or single-heartedness) *and purity of devotion to Christ."* Jesus is looking for single-hearted lovers, with eyes only for Him. He is not looking for legalistic lovers who will do all the right things and obey all the right rules.

We must realize that back in the garden of Eden, Eve did not make a simple mistake that angered God: "Okay, Eve. You made a wrong choice. You blew it! Now get out of my garden." It's much deeper than that! Eve "cheated" on God. Let this sink in. She had an affair of the heart. Eve saw something more *"pleasing to the eye"* (Gen. 3:6 NIV) than God. This object of desire took hold of her heart and led her astray from a love affair with God. This was the match that lit the fire in the garden.

He is not looking for legalistic lovers who will do all the right things and obey all the right rules

Our responsibility is to protect our minds and hearts from being deceived in the same way. Let's learn from Eve: don't let the "fruit" in life become more pleasing to your eyes than a holy love affair.

Through these three weddings it is easy to see that Jesus is crazy in love with His creation. All He ever wanted was you. Stop and let this sink deep into your spirit. Think about this during your next devotional time with the Lord. All He ever wanted was you! Focus on this when you sing a worship song and see if it changes your heart. All He ever wanted was *you!*

Jesus is not coming back for His brother, son, distant cousin, or an acquaintance. He is coming back for a bride —*His* bride. The book of Revelation tells us: *"Blessed are those who are called to the **marriage supper** of the Lamb!"* (Rev. 19:9 NKJ, emphasis added). Jesus is inviting us to a *"marriage* *supper"* for a wife who *"has made herself ready"* (Rev. 19:7 NKJV).

This is not a metaphor. This is real. This is exciting! Are you ready?

> *Then one of the seven angels ... came to me and talked with me, saying,* **"Come, I will show you the bride, the Lamb's wife."** (Rev. 21:9 NKJV, emphasis added)

13

YADA YADA YADA

Some of us are like the two women who were standing in front of me in a grocery store in a small town. They began talking about some celebrities they'd read about in the tabloids. They said, "Did you hear about this one? That one is having a baby, and have you heard that the other one got married a day after the divorce was final? I heard that one's got cancer."

If I didn't know better, I would have thought those women knew all those celebrities intimately. In fact, they didn't know them at all. All their "intimate knowledge" came from the supermarket tabloids! Their compulsive collection of suspect secondhand "facts" created a false sense of intimacy with celebrities. **Sometimes our compulsive collection of secondhand facts about God can create a false sense of intimacy with deity.**

—Tommy Tenney, The God Catchers [1]

~

*Now Adam **knew** (yada) Eve his wife, and she conceived and bore Cain.*

(Gen. 4:1 NKJV, emphasis added)
*So let us **know** (yada), let us press on to **know** (yada) the* Lord.
(Hos. 6:3 NASU, emphasis added)

T hrough the door of marriage, a special thing happens: you get to "know" your spouse. You become intimately connected in a way that no one else is allowed. This deep, intimate knowing in the Hebrew language is called *yada*. *Yada* is a specific and unique word used to describe "knowing" and crucial to understanding what a covenant relationship is. *Yada* refers to more than a mental understanding—it "denotes a knowledge that is **experiential**."[2] This "experiential" knowing goes beyond factual or mental knowledge.

Here are some interesting facts about my wife: her favorite color is blue, she loves Canadian-bacon on pizza and she grew up in Minnesota. Now you know my wife. Well, at least you know a few facts about her. But you don't really know her. I learned these things during our first few dates, but these details are not what make her tick. My journey of getting to know her better and more intimately has been a process of *yada*. I'm so glad that I wasn't content with the surface details of her life; otherwise, I would have missed the life-changing joy of true intimacy.

Some people in the church make the same mistake with Jesus, thinking that if they know enough "facts" about Him they will experience intimacy with Him. Sadly, this usually leads to frustration and disappointment that may result in either leaving Him or being satisfied with religion instead of true friendship.

Genesis 4:1 states that Adam *"knew"* (yada) Eve. The word

yada was used to refer "to a **total relationship**, emotional as well as sexual. A more accurate translation would be: 'Adam attached himself to Eve his wife.'"[3] This is not a term that simply refers to a sexual relationship; otherwise, a different Hebrew word would have been used. Instead, *yada* was used to describe a level of intimacy and commitment that goes beyond physical contact. I believe Abraham Heschel described *yada* best when he states that *yada* involves the "**attachment of the whole person.**"[4]

This mirrors our relationship with God. *Vine's Expository Dictionary* states, "To know God (*yada*) is to have an **intimate experiential knowledge** of Him."[5] This phrase is the heart of *yada*. This is the longing of God. Words are almost too limiting when trying to describe the ultimate knowing, the ultimate connection that *yada* represents.

But this is what He is inviting us into: "intimate experiential knowledge of Him." *Yada* is such a unique word and concept that if one pursues its true understanding, even just by meditating on what it means, it will change the way you relate to Jesus. It will also give you a clearer understanding of how He sees you and wants to develop a deeper friendship with you. That is priceless!

Adam could have known and memorized every fact about Eve, but they would have birthed no children. We can know all the facts about Christ, even memorize Bible passages about Him, but still not have an "intimate experiential knowledge" of Him.

This is why we were created— to experience His love, not just understand it.

Attaching our whole person to God is what changes us. This is what makes life meaningful. This is why we were created— to *experience* His love, not just understand it.

There is a difference, even a tension, between intimate (interior) knowledge and mental (exterior) knowledge; it is relational vs. factual. Of course, factual knowledge is not wrong; it is very important. Factual knowledge can help lead us into a deeper experience with the one we are learning about. But there's a problem when our minds are tricked into thinking that factual knowledge is the same as an intimate, life-changing friendship. If I thought that knowing what my wife prefers on her pizza was the completion of intimacy, I would have been sadly mistaken. I would have missed the experience of knowing and experiencing her in a much more satisfying way. Likewise, knowing what God's favorite "color" is will not change your heart.

As we ponder our walk with the Lord, we need to ask ourselves: *Is there a covenant—a marriage commitment—involved in my relationship with the Lord? Is there an "I do!" in my heart toward Him?* That will help determine if we are going to experience *yada* or not. When we make a true marriage commitment, one that is in it for better or for worse, we open the door to real intimacy. This process involves complete openness and vulnerability and a willingness to sacrifice all for the One we love. On the other hand, if we are not willing to give ourselves wholeheartedly, then we are on a casual date, not wanting to pay the cost required for a real marriage.

∼

There is a truth that I don't want us to miss: *Yada* in the natural world between a husband and wife is a perfect illustration of the type of heart to heart connection He desires to have with us. The best qualities of marital love provide us with a window into spiritual realities. It's the ultimate picture of God's desire for us.

Within this parallel about marriage is a critical principal about intimacy. Getting married is more than a physical act. Marriage represents something spiritual and mysterious between two people becoming one in true intimacy, with nothing held back, nothing hidden, true and total abandonment. This is the heart of *yada*. In the same way, Jesus is calling out to the church saying, "I want that same commitment from your heart. I want the two of us to become one in true intimacy, with nothing held back, nothing hidden, true and total abandonment."

The best qualities of marital love provide us with a window into spiritual realities

This is the ultimate reason for creation—our Creator desires to experience *yada* with us!

∾

Marriage bespeaks a higher reality—the love of Christ for his church, and her joyful deference to him—and is itself enriched by what it bespeaks. Marriage is not just another mutation of human social evolution, like democracy. It is a divine creation, intended to reveal the ultimate romance guiding all of time and eternity. . . . And this is why every faithful and loving marriage is precious to God; it shines with the light of Christ's love for his people, and of their devotion to him, in the darkness of this present evil age.

Pastorally, the biblical story lifts up before us a vision of God as our Lover. The gospel is not an imperialistic human philosophy making overrated universal claims; the *gospel sounds the voice of our Husband who has proven his love for us and who calls for our undivided love in return. **The gospel reveals that, as we look out into the universe, ultimate reality is not cold, dark, blank space; ultimate reality is romance**. . . .*

*More than our popular churches and institutions and movements, **God wants us ourselves.** He wants our hearts, our loyalty, our love for himself alone. He wants to find in us the same sense of intimate belonging to Him that is appropriate to sexual union on the human level. **More than our showing the world how "relevant" the church can be, God wants us to show Him how much we treasure Him above all else.** He wants to find in us the same sense of identification with Him that is appropriate to human marriage.*[6]

Take time to ponder this truth. Contemplate the mystery of two becoming one in marriage (Eph. 6:31–32), then apply it to your walk with Christ. Discover the real reason He created you and let that insight redesign your spiritual journey forever.

*God isn't calling us into an intellectual dialogue, although He does interact with the intellect He gave us. He is calling us into a continuous and persistent passionate relationship that He characterized as a marriage between a heavenly Bridegroom and His bride, the church. . . . Platonic or passionless relationships are a Greek idea; **the passionate lifelong relationship of husband and wife was God's idea**.*[7]

14

WANDERING PASSIONS

O ne basic yet essential ingredient of a healthy marriage is passion. During my teenage years in church youth groups, the topic of having passion for Jesus seemed to be in vogue. The emphasis on this term usually revolved around the area of excitement. We were encouraged to be "excited" for Jesus, Bible reading, or sharing our faith with others. The underlying message seemed to be that passion equaled excited feelings—and if you did not have these types of feelings for Jesus, your salvation was in question. Passion was therefore pigeon-holed into how you felt on the inside, combined with how you expressed yourself on the outside.

I cannot tell you how many times I heard preachers screaming and shouting with excitement about Jesus when I was young. And in their exuberance, they proudly exclaimed that if you weren't pumped up as they were, then you were not as committed to Jesus as they were. Interestingly, some of these same people left the ministry because of major character flaws that enthusiasm could not cover. It took me many years to realize that excitement on the outside is mostly about one's personality, not about one's commitment.

Anyone who has been in a long-term relationship knows that passion must go beyond having excited feelings for someone. Moving past a shallow, Sunday-only relationship with Jesus requires authentic passion. But if we define this only as a feeling, it won't take us far. It's a mistake to equate being excited or emotional about God as the same as having passion for Him. We need to have a deeper understanding of what it really means to be an ardent lover of Christ.

The basic Latin definition of "passion" speaks of devotion so intense that it is willing to suffer or sacrifice. This parallels the Passion Week, which looks at the sufferings of Christ. So, in the basic sense of the word, what you sacrifice or suffer for is what you are passionate about. To discover what we are truly passionate about, we need to take an inventory of what we sacrifice for on a consistent basis. This type of exercise is not about putting a guilt trip on anyone; instead, it's about finding areas in our lives that clog up our pursuit of intimacy with Christ.

The things we sacrifice for are the things we do as a natural part of our daily lives, sometimes without realizing it. It's the fruit of our lives. I've heard it said, "Show me your calendar and checkbook, and I'll show you what your passions are." Look at what you spend your time, money, and energy on, and you will discover what you are willing to sacrifice for. Usually, these are not the things you force yourself to do but that you want to do.

Healthy sacrifice is not about coercion nor about being manipulated or coerced into doing something. My old understanding of sacrifice in the church usually involved leaders bashing people over the head with the Bible, telling them to suffer more for Jesus to prove their love for Him. This type of "old-time religion" says that if you love God, you will do what you hate or what you are afraid of doing to prove your love for Him. And the more difficult the sacrifice, the more God will reward you for the sacrifice. Likewise, if you aren't willing to make such sacrifices, then beware because God might make you do them. So be prepared to become a missionary in the jungles of Africa to show your true passion for God.

Does this sound like a savior you would want to be married to? Sadly, these same people usually have an unhealthy concept of the "fear of the Lord." This twisted concept of a mean and scary God who wants you to prove yourself to Him in an unholy way is not the lovesick, passionate Jesus that I know, love, serve, and trust.

Catch this: we were created in God's image (Gen. 1:27). His DNA is to sacrifice for what He loves, which is us—and He did! The good news of the gospel is that we are the objects of His passion—thus the cross! In the same way, He designed us to sacrifice for what we love. This is how we are fashioned. Therefore, I won't need unhealthy coercion to sacrifice for what I am passionate about because it's already in my DNA.

> *The good news of the gospel is that we are the objects of His passion–thus the cross!*

A perfect example of healthy passion in the natural realm is my marriage: I have more passion for my wife than any other person does, so I will gladly sacrifice more for her than anyone else on this planet. No one must coerce or shame me into sacrificing for her. I gladly give her my all.

We sacrifice every day for the things we love and enjoy doing. There was a time in my life when I was passionate about woodworking. How do I know this? Because I would sacrifice my time, money, and energy for it. At one time, I had at least eight magazine subscriptions on the topic. I could spend hours out in my shop working and not even notice time slip by. No one had to force me to sacrifice; I wanted to do it—just ask my wife.

But sacrifice does take determination. For example, my wife and I love to watch tennis on TV. Several years ago, after watching Wimbledon, we were inspired to learn how to play tennis together. With great excitement, we went to the store and bought racquets and balls. In my mind's eye, I could see the balls flying over the net with precision, just like some of the players we saw on TV. After about twenty minutes on the tennis court, we decided to take the racquets back to the store. They didn't work! (At least that is what I told myself.)

I realized there is a big difference between *watching* tennis (even with excitement and enthusiasm) and being passionate enough to learn how to *play* tennis. Learning something new requires more than an exciting feeling; it requires persistent determination to see things through.

I've done this in my relationship with Jesus as well. At times, I've been content to "watch" Him, thinking I was being passionate for Him, when I really wasn't. It's an easy mistake to think that *wanting* intimacy is the same as *pursuing* intimacy. Wanting deeper friendship is only the beginning. When I finally started swinging the racquet a few times in my spiritual life, I began to learn what true passion in a covenant relationship means. The great thing is that even though I have hit more balls out of bounds than I care to count, Jesus loves my attempts and encourages me to keep on swinging. My game might look clumsy at times, but I can't lose with Him on my side!

~

There is an old business saying, "Do what you love to do, and the money will follow." This is such an insightful saying because it speaks to the way God wired us. We will sacrifice our time, money, and energy (including our thought life) for the things we love. In the business world, this usually equals success. The same is true for relationships.

Whether you realize it or not, you are already sacrificing for many things in life. The question is: What are they? Since all people are limited in the amount of time, money, and energy one must spend, it is important to take an inventory of our passions so we can evaluate where they are being spent. Ask yourself what are you spending your passion on. If you want to have more passion in your relationship with Christ, you might have to cut back on other expenditures in life for this to happen. It is like a budget analysis: you must identify where you are overspending before you can fix the problem. Consider evaluating a few areas to help give insight and context to this evaluation.

The first area to evaluate are our treasures. The things we treasure and value in life are the things we are passionate about. By nature, we sacrifice for what we treasure. Because of this, we must be careful of what becomes our treasure. Jesus emphasizes this when He states, *"For where your **treasure** is, there will your **heart** be also"* (Luke 12:34 NASB, emphasis added). In the Greek language, *"heart"* is used to describe "the center and seat of spiritual life . . . as it is the fountain and seat of the **thoughts, passions, desires, appetites, affections, purposes, and endeavors**."[1] In other words, the heart is the core of who we are.

Jesus is declaring that whatever is important to you, whatever is precious to you, whatever you treasure, there is where your heart ("thoughts, passions, desires," etc.) will be. If you can identify what you sacrifice your time, money, and energy on, you will be able to understand your heart better. You will be able to see the true focus of your inner life. Your sacrifice is connected to what you treasure, and what you treasure exposes your heart.

∾

Another area to evaluate is worship. Worship is merely ascribing worth to something. You worship what you treasure, and your treasures are always connected to your heart. Generally, people view worship in terms of singing songs to the Lord, but there are many different types of and layers to worship. Let's look at two of those layers.

I believe that the first area of worship we might overlook is when we give worth (extra attention and energy) to people, circumstances, and events that affect us deeply. We can give this extra attention positively or negatively. Obviously, it's a normal part of life to have many different things come our way. Still, if we don't steward how we react and how much these events affect our inner life, we inadvertently sidetrack our inner peace with Jesus and are left clueless as to why.

You can learn a lot about yourself by paying attention to how much you react to events in your life. For example, pay attention to anger. Anger is a huge form of worship. Situations or people that irritate us and make us mad or frustrated are things we ascribe too much worth to. (In the same way, worrying and coveting are also forms of worship.) If these areas are ignored or not dealt with, our pursuit of a deeper relationship with Christ will be hampered.

Satan, the enemy of our souls, loves to use this type of worship to keep us from breaking through to a more intimate walk with the Lover of our souls. He wants to keep our inner thought life pre-occupied with anything or anyone that can keep us distracted so that we can't enter His secret place. *We lose the ability to taste eternity.* Instead, we eat the dirt of the external part of life, which distorts and dampens our taste buds for the real Bread of Life (see Chapter 3 about external versus eternal).

Hopefully, identifying anger or frustration as a form of worship will awaken you to redirect your attention back to the only One who deserves true worship and affection, thus taking the sting out of the situation.

The other layer of worship involves pursuit. What you seek or pursue is also what you ascribe worth to (i.e., worship). We chase after, not just sing about, what we value and worship the most. Pursuing your dreams, and better yet, pursuing your Lover, is a form of worship. Worship becomes a pursuant lifestyle, not just a Sunday activity. (See Chapters 10 and 15 for more on seeking.)

~

That God made man to be His friend appears from the third chapter of Genesis, where we find God walking in the garden in the cool of the day, looking for Adam to join Him and share His company (Gen. 3:8). That, despite sin, God still wants *human friends appears from Christ's statement that God seeks true worshippers (Jn. 4:23); **for worship, the acknowledging of worth, is an activity of friendship at its highest (hence "with my body I thee worship" in the marriage service).** God wants men to know the joy of the love-relationship from which worship springs, and of the worship itself in which that relationship finds its happiest expression.*[2]

In closing, here is my definition of passion, simplified:

- What you seek after is what you worship.
- What you worship is what you treasure.
- What you treasure is what you will sacrifice for.
- What you sacrifice for is what you are passionate about.

The question here is: **What are you passionate about?** This is important to answer if you want to grow. What are you sacrificing for on a continual basis? What are the longings of your heart connected to? Be honest and take an in-depth inventory of your life. Evaluate these things because there you will find your treasures. They aren't hiding. Likewise, look at what dominates your thought life; try to pinpoint what you are "worshiping." New levels of freedom are waiting for you.

If you want to change your priorities in life—your passions—just ask Jesus. He is more than willing to help.

15

DRIVING IN THE DITCH

For this reason I say to you, do not be worried about your life, as to what you will eat or what you will drink; nor for your body, as to what you will put on. Is not life more than food, and the body more than clothing?
*Do not worry then, saying, "What will we eat?" or "What will we drink?" or "What will we wear for clothing?" For the Gentiles **eagerly seek** all these things; for your heavenly Father knows that you need all these things. **But seek first** His kingdom and His righteousness (My interpretation: in other words, **restore the first commandment back to first place**), and **all these things** will be added to you.*
—*Matthew 6:25, 31–33 NASU, emphasis added*

G rowing up in church, I was taught that if something wasn't going right in life, the answer was to "seek" God more (i.e., pray harder, read the Bible more, give more money, etc.). Or if things were going right, but I wanted a specific prayer answered, the solution was simple: go after God more. In other words, seek God more and better and then "all these things would be added to"—*me*! At least that was my hope, anyway. The opposite was also taught as true: if things weren't going my way, then I was doing something wrong; I wasn't seeking God enough or in the right way.

Without realizing it, we sometimes seek God as a means to an end, hoping to get "all these things" added to our lives. Please let me qualify once again: He loves for us to enjoy all these things. But because our focus is off-kilter, we don't reap the fruit of seeking that we discussed in Chapter 10. In this passage, Jesus is trying to redirect our focus. He is saying to us, "Don't be anxious over those things (what you will eat, wear, etc.) but be 'anxious' for Me. Don't seek after those things, but seek Me wholeheartedly!"

Some time ago, I experienced a major paradigm shift in my faith that changed my life. This shift set me free in ways that has helped me stay more balanced in my walk with Jesus, keeping me from driving off the road into the spiritual ditches of life. I have heard many teachings about faith, some good and some bad. It seemed that most of these teachings either emphasized where faith could take you or what faith could get you. What else if faith really for?

But one night, while reading Hebrews 11, the Lord highlighted part of verse 6 that changed the focus—changed the heartbeat—of my faith life forever.

Hebrews 11:6 says, *"And without faith it is impossible to please God, because anyone who comes to him must believe that he exists and that **he rewards those who earnestly seek him**"*

After believing that God is who He says He is, which is part of Salvation 101, the next building block of faith is to *"earnestly seek him."* In other words, the foundation of faith should be about the pursuit of Him, which is the heart of restoring the first commandment to first place in our lives. It's the essence of a love affair.

Jesus loves a passionate seeker. He rewards the heart that is chasing after Him. The foundation of faith needs to be built upon this chase. This involves turning our hearts, passions, and desires towards Him in a fresh way every day. We are to fix our *"eyes"* on Jesus, who is the *"author and perfector of our faith"* (Heb. 12:2 NIV).

Here is what is so unique about this kind of seeking: it's about the chase of one lover toward another; it's based on *two* who want to become *one*. This is the heart of Hebrews 11:6. Seeking that is based on a heart-to-heart relationship is what really changes you; it refreshes and replenishes you instead of draining you dry. This is the bedrock of faith.

And the reward mentioned in verse 6 is what happens when you find the One you are seeking: you get more of Him! Yes, you will see other things happen as well, but the true reward is a closer relationship. Just like I experience more of my wife's heart when I pursue her, the same is true in the Spirit. And He loves to be found! If you want more, you get more.

~

Unfortunately, I believe in our haste to get our prayers answered or to get "all these things" (Matt. 6:33), we take the pursuit of a love affair for granted, which undermines the foundation of true faith. When this happens, unknowingly, we look at faith as a technique for solving a problem or getting a new car (even though I believe in having faith for such). I call this "code faith" — faith that looks for the right code or pin number to God's bank account. This could also be called "recipe faith," reading the right "how to" books, looking for the five easy steps, or finding the right recipe to get our prayers answered. In our immaturity, the disciplines of our faith (prayer, Bible reading, fasting, giving, etc.) become ways to bargain with God instead of ways to grow deeper in intimacy with Him.

Our faith needs to be built on relationship, not on right techniques or beliefs

Because of this type of thinking, our faith becomes skewed or distorted. We seek Him first, *kind of*, but our eyes are really fixed on *"all these things."* Again, "all these things" are not the problem. Christ loves to bless us. But our immaturity and carnal nature can taint the foundation of our faith if we are not careful. *Our faith needs to be built on relationship*, not on right techniques or beliefs. **Pursuing the first commandment must be the cornerstone of faith.**

∾

When the foundation of our faith is off center, we tend to drive off the road and into a ditch, on one side or the other. Where I grew up in the Midwest, ditches are usually deep drainage trenches on each side of the road. Some of these are so deep that driving into one is usually a catastrophe.

The first ditch we need to keep from driving into is pride. Pride can sneak into our lives when we get elated with our ample faith, thinking we have figured out the right code or technique to getting our prayers answered. The other ditch we need to avoid is the opposite of pride: self-condemnation, where we feel dejected about our lack of faith if our prayers are not answered.

When we live with a wrong focus, we are easily tossed back and forth between these two extremes—pride and self-condemnation—causing emotional ups and downs. I call these faith cycles (or happiness cycles). This is just an illustration, so not everything here is cut and dried.

The word happy comes from the old English word "hap," which describes one's luck or lot in life, his fate or chance. When the "haps" or happenstances of life go a person's way, they are "happy." If someone is unlucky or their circumstances don't go a certain way, they are "unhappy." For most people, this is what life consists of—chasing after happy circumstances and avoiding the unhappy ones.

Surprisingly, most Christian's lives tend to mirror those who don't know Christ in this area. We spend our time and energy, even our faith, trying to create positive "haps" (circumstances), while feverishly trying to avoid the negative ones. Sometimes the only difference between us and the world in this pursuit is that we try to look more spiritual by adding "in the name of Jesus" to the mix.

You might be thinking, *What's wrong with that? Doesn't God want us to be happy?* What we sometimes fail to realize is that satan loves to confuse us about what really satisfies our soul. Peace and freedom found in Christ trumps the search of positive "haps." Real joy is found in having a friendship with our One true love, not in pursuing good circumstances.

Please know that I'm not against praying for good circumstances; *I'm against being controlled by them.*

The first commandment is relationship based, not happenstance based. While Jesus wants us to pray into our situations and lift our needs to Him, we can't lose focus of what true life is really about—making the "first," first.

It's a tragedy that we get excited and defeated by the same things that the world does. If we are honest with ourselves, the happenstances of life end up controlling our emotions and mood swings more than we realize. We have good days or bad days based strictly on the events in our lives. Instead of living in true *"peace and joy in the Holy Spirit"* (Rom. 14:17), we usually try to manipulate our outer world to feel a false sense of rest. This rest, however, is not real and short lived.

∿

As a side note, finding this *"peace and joy in the Holy Spirit"* can be tricky at first; it may even feel elusive and unobtainable. But like the journey in a marriage from infatuation to being truly in love, finding peace in Him alone is a process. It doesn't happen overnight. Sometimes it's two steps forward and one step back; but if you stay at it, you will see progress.

> *Amazingly, once you start to taste His peace, you become ruined for any other substitutes*

It takes time and effort to allow the Holy Spirit to help rewire your spiritual DNA in this area, to wean yourself off of the need to feel happiness through circumstances. Amazingly, once you start to taste His peace, you become ruined for any other substitutes.

∿

When we live out of balance and focus more on external happiness than inner rest, it produces what I call faith cycles or happiness cycles. The picture I have in my mind that illustrates this best is that of an EKG machine at a hospital, that shows a person's heartbeat pulsating up and down, again and again. Instead of living in God's steady, consistent peace, we let our lives mimic an EKG cycle, experiencing up and down emotional spikes based on what's going on around us, good or bad. In other words, we let the "haps" of life dictate the state of our inner world.

Praying for our problems and situations in life is obviously not wrong—I believe in praying and love seeing prayers answered. But when our main objective in our spiritual walk is getting our prayers answered or our faith to "work" for us instead of walking in something more mature and satisfying, we start to go off course. If we are consumed in our prayer life with only getting the blessings and pleasures (the positives of life), and keeping away the pain, problems, and pressures (the negatives of life), joy is no longer our goal—temporary happiness is. Unfortunately, this temporary happiness is not only short lived, but is also determined by the success or failure of those prayers.

When this shift in priorities becomes our primary focus, we open wide our heart's door to the outside influence of the world to determine the state of our inner heart. We leave His inner sanctuary in search for something more. But let me tell you a secret: that "something more" doesn't exist! Nothing can replace the secret place of Psalm 27:5.

Please know this: His joy will produce happiness, but happiness will never produce eternal joy.

With faith, we can see prayers answered. We can move mountains in this life! But the foundation of faith is not the ability to move mountains. When our focus is on whether our faith is successful or not, we allow life's situations to control us.

This lets both positive and negative circumstances dictate whether or not we are going to have a good day, week, or month. Our faith, as well as our happiness, goes on a roller-coaster ride, up one moment and down the next with each turn of events. We become like a living pinball machine, letting our inner lives get bounced around by outer circumstances.

Obviously, it is not wrong to have faith for answered prayers. But if you are tired of the emotional cost of trying to make faith work, take an inventory of what your prayer time is *consumed* with: answered prayer or experiencing a relationship.

～

Years ago, I was walking from one room to another in my house when out of nowhere, I heard a phrase go through my spirit that caught me off guard. It was so unusual that I knew it wasn't my own words. Interestingly, this phrase summarizes this battle I'm talking about.

Circumstantial peace is a false messiah. When I heard this, I instantly knew that this was no ordinary thought, but a challenging insight from the Holy Spirit.

As I started to unpack this phrase, what convicted me the most was how I unintentionally try to make positive circumstances the source of my rest and peace. When I look to getting my prayers answered **as a way of finding inner peace**, answered prayers inadvertently become my messiah rather than Jesus, who is peace personified. We need to understand that whether the prayer is answered or not, we can still have peace because we have Him! Remember—any other source of peace is a false messiah.

The challenge that I struggle with is this: In the midst of day-to-day living, which messiah do I turn to for satisfaction? Which messiah holds the key to my inner rest? Which messiah is my prayer-time consumed with? *Who* is my messiah—Jesus or my circumstances?

This journey toward something deeper with Christ does not shy away from asking for wrongs to be righted or for things in life to get better. It is His joy to bless us beyond belief. But at the same time, **we must realize that the power of rest is in the Person, not in the situation.**

∼

Why has God spoken? He is self-sufficient, and does not need men's gifts or service (Acts 17:25); to what end, then, does He bother to speak to us?

The truly staggering answer which the Bible gives to this question is that God's purpose in revelation is to make friends with us. It was to this end that He created us rational beings, bearing His image, able to think and hear and speak and love; He wanted there to be genuine personal affection and friendship, two-sided, between Himself and us – a relation, not like that between a man and his dog, but like that of a father to his son, or a husband to his wife. **Loving friendship between two persons has no ulterior motive; it is an end in itself. And this is God's end in revelation. He speaks to us simply to fulfill the purpose for which we were made; that is, to bring into being a relationship in which He is a friend to us, and we to Him, He finding His joy in**

giving us gifts and we finding ours in giving Him thanks.[1]

Look at a part of the above quote again: "Loving friendship between two persons has no ulterior motive; it is an end in itself." Wow! I sure wish someone had taught me this before I got married—and before I started my walk with Jesus. If only I had known that true friendship has no hidden agendas or motives, I would have experienced a lot less pain and confusion.

Thankfully, as we redirect our focus back onto intimacy (the first commandment), *we learn to draw our peace and joy from knowing Him, not from our circumstances.* Life lived from this foundation is freeing, and faith grows stronger and stronger. Worship and praise become more natural and freer when not based on the "haps" of life but on who He is.

When Paul tells us to *"fight the good fight of faith"* (1 Tim. 6:12), he is speaking of a fight to know Jesus more, not a fight to get more prayers answered. Maturing faith is built upon friendship and intimacy with Christ. Do yourself a favor and quit trying to keep score of your faith victories and defeats, which will throw you into spiritual ditches. Instead, fix your eyes— your affection—on Jesus. With this foundation in place, you can *"say to this mountain, 'Go, throw yourself into the sea,' and it will be done"* (Matt. 21:21 NIV). Tell your fears and worries to "go jump in a river," instead of allowing them to throw you into one.

~

Do not worry then, saying, "What will we eat?" or "What will we drink?" or "What will we wear for clothing?" For the

*Gentiles **eagerly seek** all these things; for your heavenly Father knows that you need all these things. **But seek first** His kingdom and His righteousness (in other words, **restore the first commandment back to first place**), and all these things will be added to you.* (Matt. 6:31–33 NASU, emphasis added)

We could reword Matthew 6:31–33 this way: "Do not worry about the positive or negative 'haps' in life, for the Gentiles (those who don't know Me) worry and are consumed about such things—but eagerly seek Me; pursue Me with all your heart. Restore our love-affair back to first place, and you will see amazing things added to your life."

The main question of this passage is this: what do you eagerly seek? Take an inventory of your spiritual walk. What is the priority of your prayer life? What is your faith consumed with—intimacy or answered prayers?

Please know this: **Intimacy will produce "all these things," but "all these things" will never produce intimacy.**

16

AM I ENOUGH FOR YOU?

The one who truly seeks God expects only one thing: God. He is looking for God, not just the things God can give him. **The prayer of his life is, "God, I just want You."** *When was the last time you prayed that prayer? I believe God wants to reveal Himself to us, but most of us just aren't interested.*

It has always been my contention that we share a common trait with God in relationships. Any time we begin a new relationship we are hesitant to reveal very much about who we really are....

In the same way, God is hesitant to reveal very much of Himself to any casual seeker who can "take it or leave it." However, when a person is truly interested in seeing who He is... **God will reveal Himself in dynamic ways.**[1]

—Ron Auch, Pentecostals in Crisis

Is God enough for you? What a tough question. If you casually answered, "Well, of course He is," then I'm not sure you understood the question. Is He *really* enough?

Years ago, when I was first starting this journey, I would periodically hear the Lord whisper this question into my spirit: "Am I enough for you?" It was so gentle—yet intrusive at the same time. At first this caught me off guard; then it perplexed me. *What? What does He mean?* I was confused, yet somehow, I thought I knew what He was asking. Sometimes, I would boldly proclaim, "Yes you are!" followed by a timid, "I think?" I could sense Him smile at me ever so gracefully, as only He can do—but then once again whisper ever so tenderly, "Am I really enough for you?"

I remember some restless nights over this question. It started me down some roads in my heart that, at first, I didn't want to travel. It made me open some doors I would have rather left closed, exposing motivations and attitudes that I didn't realize were there. This caused me pain and turmoil. **But once I let this question push me toward intimacy with Christ**, push me toward His freedom and forgiveness, **it became a flashlight into my life**, helping me to see the path a little more clearly.

"Am I enough for you?" In struggling with this question, please know that God does not want or expect us to exclude other relationships under the umbrella of this question. We need each other! We need healthy relationships. We need other people's wisdom and insights. We need others to help us see our own shortcomings. We need to give and sacrifice for others to experience a deeper level of love.

"Am I enough for you?" is not about excluding and rejecting others but about discovering the depths of the secret place in one's heart reserved only for Him. Jesus is jealous for that place in your life. Only He can satisfy this special place in your heart. Thus the question, thus the challenge!

This question is still one of the toughest things for me to

answer at times, and I still wrestle with it. But the struggle is worthwhile. There is life and freedom on the other side of this question.

~

One night, early in this journey of wrestling and finding some breakthroughs, we had some friends over for dinner. The husband disclosed he was depressed about life because he couldn't find fulfillment in his job, mostly because it wasn't his true calling. Instead of sitting behind a desk, he really wanted to be on the front lines in full-time ministry but felt he couldn't because of his responsibility to his family (which inadvertently made him resent his family some). Because of this, he was struggling with feeling unworthy in God's eyes and thought he was letting Him down. Disappointing God was like an anchor on his soul.

Early in this conversation, it was clear his struggle was similar to mine but wrapped in a different package. My friend thought that what we do for God would make Him happy, then the emptiness would go away—neither of which is true. On the surface, the math looks simple: "do" something for God, and everyone goes home a winner. It is so hard for us to see that intimacy does not work this way.

Throughout the evening, I asked him a few different times and in a few different ways, "Is God enough for you?" Granted, this was still so new to me that I did not communicate the heart of this question as well as I wish I could. But I also knew this was the root of his malcontent and I just wanted to help. At first he was confused and perplexed by this question: "What are you talking about?" he asked. "What are you saying?" He was taken aback by such a forward question, which looking back, I don't blame him. All I knew is that freedom could be found in the struggle with this question.

I distinctly remember toward the end of the evening, I tossed this question out one last time, hoping to help. I can't remember the context of the conversation at this point, but the look on his face said more than words. He seemed threatened, like I was questioning his salvation, asking, "What do you mean? I'm a Christian, aren't I?" I didn't say this, but the truth is that salvation does not answer this question. Let me repeat this: Salvation does not answer this question.

Interestingly, several times throughout the conversation, my friend also kept declaring, "It's God's will that I'm after!" How many times have I heard and said this myself, "It's God's will that I'm after!" This is one of those pious things we like to say, thinking we are endearing ourselves to Him the more we recite this. After years of searching, I have found that Jesus doesn't want us to find His "will," but *Him*. What kind of marriage would I have if the only thing my wife wanted of me was to find her "will" for my life?

We can be after His will, but not after Him in a personal way

Unknowingly, we can be after His will, but not after *Him* in a personal way. It's easy to confuse being after God's will with being after an intimate relationship with Him. We think of them as being the same thing, but they are not. Jesus doesn't want only our actions; He wants our hearts, and then the actions will follow in a much more authentic way.

～

Am I enough for you? Why is this such a crucial question to struggle with? Because I believe that this is really **the first commandment in question form**: *"Love the Lord your God with all your heart and with all your soul and with all your mind"* (Matt. 22:37 NIV).

The first commandment is what we are designed and created for. Everything else in life makes sense once this becomes our foundation. The first commandment is the spiritual Grand Canyon of the Bible. I have heard many people say this about the Grand Canyon: "Words cannot describe it properly, and a picture does not do it justice. Only when you see it in person does it take your breath away." This is also true of a spiritual love affair with Jesus. Words cannot describe it properly. When you catch a glimpse of the beauty of having a love affair with Jesus, it will take your breath away.

There is no greater battle, no greater philosophical or theological discovery, nothing more worth selling everything for, than to enter the wonder and beauty of this command. Interestingly, this is not a "you had better do this or else" command; that would be contradictory to true love. In truth, it's not a command at all—it's an invitation to *life!*

We need to filter everyday life through this grid. The primary battle is not how to behave a certain way, do the right thing, or to attend church every Sunday. *The primary battle in life is to discover the depth and importance—and yet the simplicity—of loving Jesus with all of our hearts.*

Everything else is secondary.

~

One of the hardest struggles in our Christian walk is recognizing the difference between knowing something in our heads and living in the reality of that truth in our hearts. It's the "head verses heart" battle we all face. It's vital to learn with our intellect, but we also need that mental truth to invade our hearts to change us; otherwise, it is mere academics. The initial "aha" moment about a truth is the beginning of the journey; it is not the maturity of that truth.

It is important that we don't fall into the same deception as the lawyer did in the Gospel of Luke:

> *On one occasion an expert in the law stood up to test Jesus. "Teacher," he asked, "what must I do to inherit eternal life?" "What is written in the Law?" he replied. "How do you read it?" He answered: "Love the Lord your God with all your heart and with all your soul and with all your strength and with all your mind"; and, "Love your neighbor as yourself." "You have answered correctly," Jesus replied. "Do this and you will live." But he wanted to justify himself, so he asked Jesus, "And who is my neighbor?" (Luke 10:25–29 NIV)*

Let me paraphrase Jesus' reply back to the lawyer in verse 28: "Great answer! You have gotten past the first hurdle; you understand this truth mentally—now go and understand it in your heart. Let it touch every fiber of your being, because when this touches your heart, you will truly live!"

But verse 29 reveals that the lawyer did not grasp the importance of this in his heart. He wasn't interested in a love affair with God (that would then affect his relationship with others); he only wanted to know what the rules were, the technical details of this "command." He wanted to test Jesus and argue doctrine so he could justify himself. This is where we can start to spot the difference between religion and relationship. A. W. Tozer writes, *"You can be straight as a gunbarrel theologically and as empty as one spiritually."* Correct theology will not give us life.

The first commandment is not a theology to be argued but a doorway to be walked through into life as He created it to be

The first commandment is not a theology to be argued but a doorway to be walked through into life as He created it to be. And the ultimate expression of this life is seen in the total commitment and sacrifice of marriage. This is reinforced with God's declaration in Hosea 2:16, that He wants to encounter us as our husband, not as a master. The reality of this verse must change us; it must transform our view of who we are to Christ and who Christ wants to be to us. If we aren't changed by this truth, then the first command is just that—a command, one we can never live up to.

The beauty of the first command is that it only takes a "yes" in our hearts to start this journey into life, love, and passion. This is not a passive mental yes, but a life-changing yes, just like in marriage.

The first commandment is Christ asking each one of us these questions:

- Will you marry me?
- Will you become one with Me?
- Am I enough for you?

∾

What man wants to be married to a woman who isn't passionately in love with him? She may cook and clean and wash with all the joy in the world, but if there isn't a passion in it, the marriage is not a healthy one. No man wants to be married to a woman like that. Well, neither does Jesus. **If we lose everything—everything—and all we're left with is Jesus, is that enough?**[2]

Am I enough for you? Let this question challenge every empty area in your life, any area where you live with frustration, uncertainty, insecurity, or emptiness. As you surrender these areas to Him, the door opens to more freedom and peace. It's okay to wrestle with the process that happens with this question, but don't stop at anything less than surrender. By surrender, I mean marriage. Like Jesus told the lawyer in Luke 10, *"Do this and* ***you will live"*** (emphasis added).

If you want to go deeper in the journey toward more intimacy, then I invite you to spend time alone with your Bridegroom and listen for these words from His heart to yours:

"You are enough for Me! I desire you like no other! Would you let ***Me*** *satisfy the longings in your heart? Would you let Me be enough for* ***you?"***

17

ADVICE FOR THE JOURNEY

H ere is a quote from a wonderful gem of a book, *The Pursuit of God* by A. W. Tozer. He gives us invaluable advice on the art of growing spiritually.

*Why do some persons "find" God in a way that others do not? Why does God manifest His presence to some and let multitudes of others struggle along in the half-light of imperfect Christian experience? Of course, the will of God is the same for all. He has no favorites within His household. All He has ever done for any of His children He will do for all of His children. **The difference lies not with God but with us.***

*Pick at random a score of great saints whose lives and testimonies are widely known. Let them be Bible characters or well-known Christians of post-biblical times. . . . They differed from the average person in that when they felt the inward longing, **they did something about it**. They acquired the lifelong habit of spiritual response. . . . As David put it neatly, "When thou saidst, Seek ye my face; my heart said unto thee, Thy face, LORD, will I seek" (Ps. 27:8).*

Receptivity is not a single thing; rather, it is a *compound, a blending of several elements within the* *soul.* *It is an affinity for, a bent toward, a sympathetic* *response to, a desire to have. . . . It may be increased by* *exercise or destroyed by neglect. . . . It is a gift of God, indeed,* *but one which must be recognized and cultivated as any other* *gift if we are to realize the purpose for which it was given.*

Let us say it again: The universal Presence is a fact. God is *here. The whole universe is alive with His life. . . . And always* *He is trying to get our attention, to reveal Himself to us, to* *communicate with us. We have within us the ability to know* *Him **if we will but respond to His overtures. (And this we*** ***call pursuing God!)** We will know Him in increasing degree* *as our receptivity becomes more perfect by faith and love and* *practice.* [1]

There are no easy answers to the pursuit of intimacy, and the journey will look different for everyone. Likewise, what works for you during one season of life might change and look different during a different season. The dance of romance always changes. Like a healthy marriage, it evolves, and hopefully the experience gets richer as time goes on.

But this journey must be taken seriously. We must respond to His gentle overtures and not take Him for granted. We must also appreciate that this journey is more of an art, and not a science— thus the wisdom in Tozer's words: "Receptivity is not a single thing; rather, it is a compound, a blending of several elements within the soul." In this chapter, I want to discuss different thoughts and principles that have helped me along the way. Of course, this list is incomplete but hopefully, a good beginning.

❧

So how do we start this journey? Start by starting. This is as profound as it gets. Don't miss this nugget of truth. Just start spending some time with Jesus the best way you know how. Talk (pray) to Jesus. Read the Bible. Ask for His help to begin the romance—just start the pursuit. Don't wait until you think you can do it the "right" way. Just start! Sometimes it is more exciting to read or talk about intimacy than actually *being* intimate with our Savior. As with any new relationship, this can feel awkward on the front end, but don't worry; Jesus is excited that you are trying. Jump into it by faith and see what happens!

> *What is crucial is that we are really on the journey, not just thinking about the journey or reading or talking about it.* **"One faltering but actual step** *is more valuable than any number of journeys performed in the imagination."* [2]

❧

This next piece of advice came from a Bible college teacher of mine, and it has stuck with me for over thirty-five years: Be free to fail! I was stunned the first time I heard this. Growing up, I never heard this message. What I heard was quite the opposite: never fail; don't ever make mistakes. Now this isn't a "be free to sin" message; instead, it's about being free to fail in reaching forward. Be free to walk this journey out, knowing that when you stumble and fall, He is right there to pick you up.

As we struggle to grow in our relationship with Christ, we

Jesus wants *you more than* *you want Him* cannot let our immaturity cause us to be discouraged and give up. Romans 8:1 gives us great news: *"Therefore, there is now **no condemnation** for those who are in Christ Jesus"* (NIV, emphasis added). When we struggle and fail, satan is right there to condemn us, telling us that we don't deserve His love and that we should give up the fight—but we can't listen to this voice.

We need to understand the difference between conviction from the Holy Spirit and condemnation from our enemy. Condemnation discourages us and brings hopelessness; it pushes us away from God through shame. Conviction draws us closer to God; it encourages us not to give up hope. The Holy Spirit lets us know that with Him, all things are possible, we can change, and we will have progress. If we can recognize the difference between these two voices, we will avoid the setbacks and ugliness of self-condemnation. Be encouraged—be free to fail in this journey.

~

Be confident in the struggle. Jesus wants you more than you want Him. Know that He is for you. You are not left alone in this journey. Sometimes the biggest part of the battle is fighting through the feelings of inadequacy and shame that the enemy keeps pushing at us. Jesus is madly in love with you! Keep pressing into His arms. Be confident in the struggle —satan hates confidence!

~

Be patient and do not give up. You are developing a deep, rich relationship with your Bridegroom King. This takes time, effort, and patience to grow, so do not lose heart. In the natural world, we have more patience with ourselves when it comes to learning a new job or a new sport than we do with our spiritual lives. Striking out in baseball or dropping a pass in football is part of the learning process, so why do we expect perfection in ourselves spiritually speaking?

We want everything to happen overnight, but it doesn't. This is about a new lifestyle, walking out a new relationship with Christ. Just like eating one nutritious meal doesn't make you healthy overnight, and one day of exercise doesn't make you fit, a new understanding of who Christ is doesn't change your heart in one day. Give it time.

> *Intimacy doesn't happen by accident*

~

Be purposeful in your pursuit of a deeper walk with Christ. **Intimacy doesn't happen by accident.** First Chronicles 22:18 says, *"Now **set** your heart and your soul to seek the LORD your God"* (NKJV, emphasis added). You will never seek the Lord without determination, without "setting" your heart to do so. In the New Testament, Paul often used action words to describe his walk with Christ. For example, in Philippians, Paul encourages us to *"**work out** your own salvation with fear and trembling"* (Phil. 2:12 NKJV, emphasis added). In other words, take it seriously. Likewise, in 1 Timothy Paul said, *"**Fight** the good fight of faith, **lay hold** on eternal life"* (1 Tim. 6:12 NKJV, emphasis added). This journey does require a "fight," one that He wants you to win!

❧

Remember that it takes two to make a marriage work—God and you. When trying to process the action words highlighted in the last section, it would be easy to feel burdened or inadequate about your ability to live out these exhortations, but don't. There is a balance. After Paul tells us to *"work out"* our salvation, he follows it with, *"[Not in your own strength] for it is God Who is all the while effectually at work in you [**energizing and creating in you the power and desire**]"* (Phil. 2:13 AMP, emphasis added).

The Christian walk is 100 percent God and 100 percent us. It is His grace and our surrender to His grace. Just remember that grace and effort are not opposites. Earning wages is the opposite of grace, but not of effort. Paul clarifies this balance: *"not having a righteousness of my own that comes from the law, but that which is through **faith** in Christ—the righteousness that comes **from God and is by faith**"* (Phil. 3:9 NIV, emphasis added). Righteousness is a free gift from God, but we must accept it and live in it by *"faith"* (see Chapter 15 for a discussion on the foundation of faith). Likewise, he states in Colossians, *"**I labor**, striving according to **His power**, which mightily works within me"* (Col. 1:29 NASB, emphasis added). This is not a one-sided relationship; it takes two to make a marriage work.

❧

This journey takes mature persistence. We must have the same moxie, the same tenacious spirit that Jacob had when he wrestled with God. He cried out to God, *"I will not let you go unless you bless me"* (Gen. 32:26 NIV). This cry, this resolve, changed Jacob's life. Wrestling to know Him more intimately will change everything about your life—your personality, your character, and your priorities. This "fight of faith" will develop maturity in us; it will also take a growing maturity to stay the course.[3]

Hosea 12:3 says something quite revealing about Jacob: *"In the womb he took his brother by the heel, And **in his maturity, he contended with God"** (Hos. 12:3 NASB, emphasis added). Please catch this: in his maturity, Jacob quit wrestling with his brother, quit wrestling to make his own way in life, quit wrestling for selfish ambitions—and started to wrestle with God, to find more of Him. It takes maturity to finally figure out what is most important in life: the fight for the first commandment. Do everything in your might to let go of immature battles. Let the cry of your heart be like Jacob's: *"I will not let you go unless you bless me."*

~

Cultivate a romance. Romance is a delicate thing to nurture, and the more you nurture it, the more it grows. Just like in a physical marriage, if you don't cultivate and protect the relationship, it will die. Of course, with God's amazing grace, it can always be resurrected! It is never too late to start over with Him. So if you want to have a special connection in your heart with Christ—even a romance—make room in your busy life for one. This will take time and effort, and maybe a few false starts, but it is worth it! Cultivate a relationship with your Bridegroom.

~

Lastly, change the way you spend your prayer time. There are three main changes in this area that have helped me.

First, we need to have a paradigm shift in our thinking as to what prayer should look like. Prayer should not involve trying to act extra holy and reverent to some big deity in the sky. It should not involve a change in your tone of voice to portray this reverence—that is religion. I can't imagine Adam doing that in the garden when he was face to face with God. Keep it real, because He is real. Likewise, prayer should not always be rattling off a list of needs and wants to God. Instead, it should be a time of give-and-take communication —*intimate* communication—as between a father and child and/or between a husband and wife, only better.

Talk to Him like you would to your closest friend. Look Jesus in the eyes and tell Him how much you love Him. Prayer is about *relating* in an intimate way to our Bridegroom King, so make it personal! Also, spend time speaking *and* listening. Let Jesus love on you, and love on Him back.

The second thing that helped jump-start my time talking with Jesus was meditating on verses in the Bible that speak of our bridal relationship with Him. I then worked that language into my heart through prayer. For example, early on, I use to pray, *"I thank you, Lord, that my Maker is my Husband"* (Isa. 54:5). I like factual statements that I can stand on in prayer to remind me of my position with Him. For example, I would declare Song of Solomon 1:2: *"May he* (the Bridegroom) *kiss me* (the Bride) *with the kisses of his mouth* (His Word).[4] *For your love is better than wine* (or any pleasure of this world). " This would remind me how special His intimacy is and bring a sense of closeness during my prayer time.

Another passage that helped my heart connect better is: *"I am my beloved's, And* **his** (Christ) **desire is for me**" (Song 7:10

NASU, emphasis added). I owned this verse and made it mine! I have repeated this verse more times than I can count. I used this to help rewire my heart into understanding that His passion and desire for me far outweighs mine. Let me encourage you to declare over and over: "His desire is for me!"

The more we realize that the Lord's desire is for us, the more our prayer life will change. Instead of hiding in shame, we open ourselves up to Him in new ways. Our expressions of love become more meaningful. The overall point here is to find verses that will change the way you see **who Christ is to you and who you are to Christ**. Then, use that new understanding to change the way you talk (pray) to Him. Like I mentioned before, you want to keep it real and personal. This will help!

Third, find romance and/or worship songs (Christian or secular) that echo your heart toward Him and His heart back to you. Turn these songs into prayers to Him. One of my favorite songs that I sing to the Lord is an old John Denver song, "Annie's Song." It expresses my feelings toward Him in a deeply fulfilling way with lyrics like: "You fill up my senses, like a night in a forest; like a mountain in springtime, like a walk in the rain." The song ends with my favorite line: "You fill up my senses, come fill me again." These types of songs help me to get away from only praying the typical "I need more money" prayers and into something deeper and more connected with Him. Find songs that will add romance to your prayer time.

∿

In closing, always remember this: *"If God is for us, who can be against us?"* (Rom. 8:31 NIV). Jesus wants us to grow in intimacy with Him more than we can imagine. The dance of romance is worth the effort. Don't settle for anything less. Don't be content with religion—go after relationship. But be aware: it's addicting. The more you taste, the more you will want.

18

FINAL THOUGHTS

I want to end by repeating (from Chapter 11) one of my all-time favorite quotes:

*For centuries prior to our Modern Era, the church viewed the gospel as a Romance. . . . But our rationalistic approach to life, which has dominated Western culture for hundreds of years, has stripped us of that, leaving a faith that is barely more than mere fact-telling. Modern evangelicalism reads like an IRS 1040 form: It's true, all the data is there, **but it doesn't take your breath away.**[1]*

I hope that by now, you have a different understanding of what it means to be the bride of Christ. I also hope that understanding Jesus as our Bridegroom becomes a personal reality and that this truth will no longer be a distant metaphor with little meaning. May the person of Jesus Christ "**take your breath away.**"

I pray that you will have the same attitude as the bride in the Song of Solomon when she cries out, *"I must seek him whom my soul loves."* Then she states, *"When I found him whom my soul loves; I held on to him and would not let him go"* (Song 3:2, 4 NASB). May this same resolve and fervor be the passion of your heart. As you discover more and more of Christ, hold on, and never let Him go!

May searching for the first and greatest commandment become the treasure hunt of your life; may you "sell" everything in life to discover the true riches of this command. May this journey not be a theory or a doctrinal understanding but a practical reality—a living, joyful, and intimate reality with Jesus.

Finally, may you struggle and grapple with what I believe to be the most important question Jesus is asking the church today.

"Will you marry Me?"

ABOUT THE AUTHOR

Gary Chiles has been married for over 30 years to his wife, Beth, and they have two children, Lily and Leland. They reside in Waco, Texas.

Gary is available for speaking engagements. To learn more go to his website at www.GaryChiles.com.

NOTES

2. The Whisper of Romance

1. Ruis, David, *True Love: Winds of Worship, Vol. 3,* (Mercy/Vineyard Publishing), 1994.
2. John Fischer. "Beggar." *Dark Horse.* Album. Myrrh Records/Word Records. 1982.

5. First Things First

1. Francis Schaeffer, The Complete Works of Francis A. Schaeffer: A Christian Worldview, 5 vols. (Westchester, Ill., Crossway Books, 1982), 4:135.

7. How Hungry Are You?

1. Tommy Tenney, *The God Catchers* (Nashville, Tenn.: Thomas Nelson Publishers, 2000), 29.

10. The Chase Is On

1. Brennan Manning, *Signature of Jesus* (Sisters, Ore.: Multnomah Books, 1996), 210.
2. *Vine's Expository Dictionary of Biblical Words,* Copyright © 1985, Thomas Nelson Publishers.
3. Abraham Heschel, *God in Search of Man: A Philosophy of Judaism* (New York: Stratford Press, Inc., 1955), 28.
4. *The Online Bible Thayer's Greek Lexicon and Brown Driver & Briggs Hebrew Lexicon,* (Woodside Bible Fellowship, Ontario, Canada, Copyright © 1993).
5. Heschel, *God in Search of Man,* 146.
6. Biblesoft's *New Exhaustive Strong's Numbers and Concordance with Expanded Greek-Hebrew Dictionary.* Copyright © 1994, 2003, 2006 Biblesoft, Inc.

7. *The Online Bible Thayer's Greek Lexicon and Brown Driver & Briggs Hebrew Lexicon* (Woodside, Bible Fellowship, Ontario, Canada, Copyright © 1993).
8. Mary Jane Klimisch, *The One Bride* (New York: Sheed and Ward, 1965), 61–62.

11. Covenant of Love

1. Manning, *The Signature of Jesus*, 212.
2. Brent Curtis and John Eldredge, *The Sacred Romance: Drawing Closer to the Heart of God* (Nashville, Tenn.: Thomas Nelson Publishers, 1997), 45.
3. *Encyclopedia Judaica Vol. 5* (Jerusalem: Keter Publishing House Ltd., 1971), 1022.
4. Raymond C. Ortlund Jr., *God's Unfaithful Wife: A Biblical Theology of Adultery* (Grand Rapids, Mich.: William B. Eerdmans Publishing Company, 1996), 146.
5. J. I. Packer, *Knowing God* (Downers Grove, Ill.: InterVarsity Press, 1973), 154.
6. From a sermon titled: *God: The Wild Lover* by Pastor David Johnson (Church of the Open Door; Minneapolis, MN).
7. Michael Kaufman, *Love, Marriage, and Family in Jewish Law and Tradition* (Northvale, N.J.: Jason Aronson Inc., 1992) 124–125.

12. Crazy in Love

1. Rabbi Aryeh Kaplan, *Made in Heaven: A Jewish Wedding Guide* (New York/Jerusalem: Moznaim Publishing Corporation, 1983), 10.

13. Yada Yada Yada

1. Tenney, *The God Catchers*, 106–107.
2. *Evangelical Dictionary of Biblical Theology*. Copyright 1996 by Baker Books.
3. Abraham Heschel, *The Prophets* (New York: The Jewish Publication Society of America, 1962), 58.
4. Heschel, *The Prophets*, 57.
5. *Vine's Expository Dictionary of Biblical Words* (Thomas Nelson Publishers).
6. Raymond C. Ortlund Jr., *God's Unfaithful Wife: A Biblical Theology of Adultery* (Grand Rapids, Mich.: William B. Eerdmans Publishing Company, 1996), 173, 176.

7. Tenney, *The God Catchers*, 166.

14. Wandering Passions

1. *Thayer's Greek Lexicon*, Electronic Database. Copyright © 2000, 2003, 2006 by Biblesoft, Inc.
2. J. I. Packer, *God Has Spoken* (Grand Rapids, Mich.: Baker Book House, 1989), 50.

15. Driving in the Ditch

1. Packer, *God Has Spoken*, 50.

16. Am I Enough for You?

1. Ron Auch, *Pentecostals in Crisis* (Green Forest, Ark.: New Leaf Press, Inc., 1988), 114.
2. Source unknown.

17. Advice for the Journey

1. A.W. Tozer, *The Pursuit of God*. (Wheaton, Ill.: Tyndale House Publishers, 1982), pp. 66–71.
2. Manning, *Signature of Jesus*, 226.
3. See Philippians 3:14–15; Hebrews 6:1.
4. See Deuteronomy 8:3.

18. Final Thoughts

1. Curtis and Eldredge, *The Sacred Romance*, 45.

www.ingramcontent.com/pod-product-compliance
Lightning Source LLC
LaVergne TN
LVHW051410080426
835508LV00022B/3016